Beauty in the Making

LEARNING TO RADIATE
FROM THE INSIDE OUT

ISIS SMALLS

Scriptures are from the following sources:

Scripture quotations noted AKJV are from The Authorized (King James) Version. Rights in the Authorized Version in the United Kingdom are vested in the Crown. Reproduced by permission of the Crown's patentee, Cambridge University Press.

Scripture quotations marked (AMP) are taken from the Amplified Bible, Copyright © 1954, 1958, 1962, 1964, 1965, 1987 by The Lockman Foundation. Used by permission.

Scripture quotations noted ASV are then from the *American Standard Version.*

Scripture quotations marked (ESV) are from the ESV® Bible (The Holy Bible, English Standard Version®), copyright © 2001 by Crossway, a publishing ministry of Good News Publishers. Used by permission. All rights reserved.

Scripture quotations marked HCSB®, are taken from the Holman Christian Standard Bible®, Copyright © 1999, 2000, 2002, 2003, 2009 by Holman Bible Publishers. Used by permission. HCSB® is a federally registered trademark of Holman Bible Publishers.

Scripture notes ISV are taken from *The Holy Bible: International Standard Version*® Release 2.1 Copyright © 1996-2012 The ISV Foundation. ALL RIGHTS RESERVED INTERNATIONALLY.

Scripture quotations noted KJV are taken from the *King James Version* of the Bible.

Scripture quotations marked MSG are taken from THE MESSAGE, copyright © 1993, 1994, 1995, 1996, 2000, 2001, 2002 by Eugene H. Peterson. Used by permission of NavPress. All rights reserved. Represented by Tyndale House Publishers, Inc.

Scripture noted NASB are taken from the New American Standard Bible® (NASB), Copyright © 1960, 1962, 1963, 1968, 1971, 1972, 1973, 1975, 1977, 1995 by The Lockman Foundation. Used by permission. www.Lockman.org

Scripture quotations marked (NIV) are taken from the *Holy Bible, New International Version*®, NIV®. Copyright © 1973, 1978, 1984, 2011 by Biblica, Inc.™ Used by permission of Zondervan. All rights reserved.

Scripture quotations noted NLT are taken from the Holy Bible, New Living Translation, Copyright © 1996, 2004, 2015 by Tyndale House Foundation. Used by permission of Tyndale House Publishers Inc., Carol Stream, Illinois 60188. All rights reserved.

Printed in the United States of America
First Printing, 2017
Isis Smalls Publishing
www.isissmalls.com
LCCN:
ISBN:

PRAISES FOR

"Beauty in the Making"

"Beauty in the Making" was written for such a time as this. It is packed with wisdom, inspiration, and biblical truths to help young women dispel the lies they are bombarded with daily, recognize their true value, and reach their full potential. I am honored to recommend both the book and the author, Isis Smalls. Isis is an extraordinarily gifted woman of God. To say that she's "all that!" would be an understatement, but it's true. She's a beautiful, intelligent, radiant, and anointed daughter of the King who's on a mission to introduce her heavenly Father to young women who don't truly "know" Him. Each page of "Beauty in the Making" is evidence of Isis' personal relationship with God. Unlike many authors, she's not writing about what she's heard or researched. She's sharing lessons from her own faith journey, one that has experienced many twists, turns, and transitions but remains on course and on purpose. It is my prayer that countless young women around the world will read this book and begin to experience the true power of God's love and the "limitless living" He promises each of His daughters."

— Barbara Curtis
Senior Director of Volunteer Development
Lakewood Church, Houston, Texas
Founder and President, RARE Pearls, Inc.

"A powerful message for girls! As a mother of two daughters ages 12 and 18, I can say that this book will bless girls of any age with practical wisdom, inspiration and encouragement to live to her full potential! Isis brings much needed insights to young women on how to live a Christ-centered life in a world where they are being bombarded by social media. What a treasure!"

— Suzie Austin
Pastor's wife, Mother of 2 daughters, Realtor

"In just the first few paragraphs, it's easy to see that Beauty in the Making is destined to be an instant classic, a coming-of-age companion for young girls who know they are called to be more than what is prescribed to them on the pages of glossy magazines. Isis Smalls bravely exposes her most vulnerable moments and shares insights from her most potent victories in order to inspire her readers to fiercely embrace their faith, courageously face their fears and dare to be set apart! Parents, are you looking to raise bold, brave, fiercely feminine young ladies who pray without ceasing and know who they are in Christ? Then get this book in your daughter's hands pronto!"

— Jade Simmons
Powerhouse Speaker & International Concert Pianist
Author of "Audacious Prayers for World Changers"
www.jadesimmons.com

"Beauty in the Making is a powerfully anointed book full of practical teaching that I have thoroughly enjoyed going through with my daughter. I finally found the right resource to help me teach my tween daughter how to live according to biblical principles. I highly recommend this book!"

— Pastor Steve Austin
Senior Director of Pastoral Care
Lakewood Church, Houston, Texas

"Beauty in the Making: Learning to Radiate from the Inside Out floats like a butterfly! It's alive and it is free-flowing! Just like a butterfly's beautiful wings are actually transparent, through sharing many of her personal testimonies and lessons learned, Isis is open and honest. Her authenticity teaches young women how to shine in the midst of becoming. Like a caterpillar in its metamorphosis, as the monarch is flexible and open, she is sure to soar! This highly anointed All-American athlete and beauty queen demonstrates that there are no borders in which God confines His purpose or people. Daughters of the King learn how to taste and see that He is good. As they stand on God's Word, His sustenance, they discover that life is limitless!"

— Pamela-Faye
Beloved and Unique Daughter of King Yeshua

"Isis Smalls has given us a blueprint for rearing our daughters to know their worth and value in God. Every young woman who practices the principles of this book, will thank the author years later."

— Frederick D. Jones, J.D.
Founder and President
Publish Me Now University
Write Your Worth Academy
www.drfredjones.com

DEDICATION

To my fierce family of faith-filled, audacious, and ambitious superheroes....Jerome Smalls, Loretta Smalls, and Jade Simmons: I love you. Thank you for making the concept of "dreaming big" more than a motto in my life. Thank you for teaching me that fulfilling my potential has everything to do with loving and serving people and becoming all God wants me to be in the process. For that, I am forever grateful.

Isis

CONTENTS

Part 4

GIRL ON A MISSION: Limitless Living with God 99

FOREWORD

I've heard it said that big minded people make you feel big! When I met Isis Smalls I knew had a friend who could agree with me on any magnificent dream God put in my heart to accomplish. She thinks big, believes big, and sees each individual as a potential candidate for greatness. Whether it was during her time as a member of our Lakewood Church Choir or during her reign as Miss Houston 2014, Isis operated with bold faith, unshakeable integrity, and an inspiring love for God. I have been so privileged to personally watch Isis chase after God while working out her faith, tackling adversity, and staying faithful when there were plenty of opportunities to compromise.

For this I must accredit her devotion to Jesus. She thinks big because she knows her God is well able. She believes big because she trusts His heart. She sees big in others because she herself has watched God take her through the process of trusting Him and believing in his promises. She knows first hand what God can do with a willing heart and she so beautifully shares these experiences with us in *Beauty in the Making: Learning to Radiate from the Inside Out*."

The keys to her success, inner strength, and fortified foundation are found in this book. As you read through these pages, you will be inspired to live courageously, boldly, and purposefully. You will learn how to bounce back when life throws you curveballs and how to own the stage when God gives you the floor. Get ready to be empowered with tools to grow in your faith, character, and confidence.

Beauty in the Making is an amazing avenue to discovering who God really is and who He has made you to be! There is no greater relationship than the one with your Maker. The more you know God, the more you will understand yourself and His purposes for your life! Take your time soaking up the wisdom and truth so carefully laid out here for you and you will undoubtedly Radiate from the Inside Out!

Fiona Mellett

Author ~ Brave & Beautiful
Music Pastor ~ Lakewood Church, Houston, Texas

PREFACE

As you journey through *Beauty in the Making: Learning to Radiate from the Inside Out*, it is my heart's deepest cry that you know what is the height, the depth, and the width of God's love for you. At the age of 26, I have experienced enough of life to tell you with confidence that God is the only person who can truly love you unconditionally. Though the people in our lives love us and mean the best for us, eventually some friends will fail. Family, although they try, will not always succeed. Boyfriends will come and go and if you're ever blessed enough to have supporters or some kind of fan base, they too can be fickle. At the end of every single day, the only thing that remains is JESUS.

We hear it preached day in and day out, that God's love is the one thing that remains. I hope that as you dive into the daily teachings of this book, that truth will begin to penetrate your heart like never before. It is my prayer that you will not just know about Jesus, but that you will also experience Him for yourself. What is so beautiful about Him is that He loves us uniquely. How God reveals Himself to you is special and divinely tailored to your heart. You will sense God's love and passion for you in ways that are fresh and true to your life and experiences.

Get ready for an adventurous ride with the One who died on the cross and gave His life for you. Oh, how He loves YOU!

Isis Smalls

Author & Youth Empowerment Speaker
"Activating Potential in Young Women"

3

Introduction

GETTING THE MOST OUT
OF YOUR JOURNEY

Beauty in the Making: Learning to Radiate from the Inside Out is intended to encourage, challenge, and strengthen you in your walk with God. The book is divided into four parts. Each chapter and section builds on the previous one, so it is recommended to read them in order.

Part 1 - You Are Loved: Developing Intimacy with God is designed to help you reflect on your personal relationship with God and to better understand your identity in Christ. When you know who you are and Whose you are, everything else in your life will begin to fall into place.

Part 2 - Heart Conditions: Checking Your Character is filled with stories from my personal life in which I am very honest and transparent. It is written to encourage you to take a good look at your character and to prayerfully bring any areas in need of growth to God.

Part 3 - Divinely Aligned: Walking in Purpose Daily is constructed to remind you that you are a woman of destiny. Your life is a necessity. You are enough and you matter. In this section, you will be inspired to discover your unique talents and gifts and learn how to use them for God.

Part 4 - Girl on a Mission: Limitless Living with God is all about living freely and fully as the woman God created you to be. You do not exist to simply survive; you were built to thrive! In this section, get equipped with the tools you need to make the most of every season in life: the good, the bad, and the downright ugly!

To make the most of your journey through this book, I suggest that you follow these steps:

1. **Pray**: Before you begin reading, invite God into your time. Ask Him to give you wisdom and understanding and to enlighten you on how to apply what you are learning.

2. **Be Intentional**: Read to absorb the material, not to simply check the day's reading off of your to-do list. Just like any of your friends, God desires to spend quality time with you. Be sure to set aside time in your day where you can read without feeling rushed and can be open to what God has to say.

3. **Reflect**: After each reading, write down your thoughts and feelings as a way to respond to what the Lord puts on your heart. Grab a journal and write what comes to you. Let it flow! Ask yourself these questions: What did I learn? What do I need to change? How did God encourage me? How did He correct me? Notes are a great way to capture what God is saying so that you do not forget!

4. **<u>Pray Again</u>:** Ask God to seal what you learn on your heart and bring it back to your remembrance when you or others may need it. Thank Him for what He has teaches you and ask Him to give you the strength and grace to apply what you learn in order to live it out in your life. Every chapter includes a "prayer starter" to get you going!

Part 1

YOU ARE LOVED:

Developing Intimacy with God

The Christian walk is more than going to church; it is about doing life with Christ. As you grow up, you will realize it is not enough to simply know <u>about</u> Jesus. Life is just too hard and too complex to walk it out alone. You have to know Him for real. You have to know Who He is for yourself. As you read through this opening section, I urge you to be honest about these questions: Is Jesus more than a character in the Bible to you? Is He a Friend you feel you can honestly turn to? Pray that God will guide you in establishing a thriving friendship with Christ. Jesus wants to walk out every day with you if you are willing to let Him in. Let's develop true intimacy with Christ.

1. Daddy's Little Girl

WHAT DOES YOUR FATHER
SAY ABOUT YOU?

John 3:16 (NIV) "For God so loved the world that He gave His one and only Son, that whoever believes in Him shall not perish, but have eternal life."

J ust like little kids days before Christmas . . .
Just like teenagers hours before a concert . . .
Just like a bride minutes before her wedding . . .
Just like an audience seconds before the big announcement . . .

God eagerly waits for you.

He smiles and sings when He thinks of you (Zephaniah 3:17).
He wants to fill your heart with gladness (Isaiah 61:3).
He knows the number of hairs on your head (Matthew 10:30).
He wants to take away your sadness (Psalm 30:11).

Before your feet even hit the floor, (Psalm 91:11)
His angels are dispatched in concern of you (Psalm 91:11).
He calls you His very own (Isaiah 43:1).
He loves you, no matter what you do (1 Timothy 1:15-16).

He has seen every one of your tears (Revelation 7:17).
He captures them in a bottle (Psalm 56:8).
He has written your name on the palms of His hands (Isaiah 49:16).
He catches you before you topple (Psalm 91:12).

He knows your past, present, and future (Jeremiah 29:11).
He uses every one of your sorrows (2 Corinthians 7:10).
He knows the desires of your heart (Psalm 37:4).
He promises you better tomorrows (Proverbs 4:18).

He loves you, dear Daughter (Romans 8:37-39).
He wants to give you the world (Psalm 84:11).
He says you are beautiful (Song of Solomon 4:7).
You are His Baby Girl (1 John 3:1).

Sometimes God seems so magnificent and mighty that it is hard to imagine that He wants to know us intimately. In the midst of all that He does in the universe, it is difficult to grasp that He still cares about our little world. But . . . it is true. He cares.

The God who put the world in motion is interested in your life . . . every single day of it! He wants to be a part of your daily activities. He wants to help you along. God has amazing plans for us and a purpose for every breath we take; but, it is our job to acknowledge Him and welcome Him into our lives. It is up to us to <u>receive</u> and <u>accept</u> the Love that He pours out on us.

Today and every day, God is telling you to take His Love personally. The Bible says in John 3:16 (NIV), "For God so loved the world that He gave His one and only son, that whoever believes in Him shall not perish, but have eternal life." He did not just give His Son for the world; He gave his Son for YOU! Hold tightly to that truth today.

Prayer Starter: Dear Precious Heavenly Father, I am absolutely amazed by Your love for me. What You have written about me is beautiful and, by faith, I fully receive it. When life gets tough, help me to remember that You love me. When I mess up, help me to know that You have forgiven me. Though the world is big and I am one of Your many children, I am determined to take Your Love personally. Thank You for all that You have done and will do for me. I will declare today and every day that I AM LOVED BY YOU!

2. Girl on a Mission

STARTING YOUR DAY OFF STRONG

Jeremiah 29:11 (NIV) "For I know the plans I have for you," declares the LORD, "plans to prosper you and not to harm you, plans to give you hope and a future."

You are a young woman of purpose and divine destiny! When you woke up this morning all of Heaven and Hell came to attention! When your feet hit the floor, your angels got into place and the Holy Spirit declared: "Let's go, girl! Let's do this!" When you are a girl after God's own heart, every day becomes an adventure! Every day God assigns you a mission. Sometimes your mission will be to simply do your best and honor God in all that you do. Other days it may be to go speak with a lonely person in the cafeteria or give the store clerk a compliment at the register. Whatever the assignment is, big or small, you are here to fulfill two purposes: Love God and Love People. That is YOUR divine mission!

Let's be real though: Loving God and loving people are not always easy. There may be seasons when you are on fire for God and excited about life. Then, there are seasons when you feel like you entered a drought or a rut that you cannot quite escape. Because life can be so up and down, you have to check in with God on a DAILY basis. He helps you remain steady and constant in the midst of life's unpredictability.

God is the Captain of your ship. He is the Pilot of your plane. He is the Tour Guide on this life adventure.

As with any good road trip, you would not hop into the car without first getting instructions. Our walk with God should be the same! Every morning, before you even leave your room, try doing this power-packed routine that I affectionately call **G.P.S**:

Moment of Gratitude
Time of Prayer
Dose of Scripture

Gratitude: The Bible tells us to be thankful in all things. It tells us that every day is one the Lord has made and we should rejoice and be glad in it! I have noticed that I am not excited about every day though. Especially if it is early in the morning, you will not find me jumping out of bed singing "Hallelujah!" I have learned, however, that even on my worse days, there is *still* something for which I can be grateful. Even if I simply thank God for giving me another day to live, for keeping me healthy and safe, or for blessing me with food to eat . . . there is something! No matter how awful your situation is, it could always be worst—maintaining a heart of gratitude will help you remain content. When you are content, the Lord will bless you with more to get happy about!

Prayer: is simply talking to God. You can tell Him everything and you can ask Him for anything. You can share what concerns you or makes worry. You can tell Him about your family, friends, your hopes, and your dreams. Nothing is off limits when it comes to talking to God. Taking time to chat with Him gives you fuel for your day and it gets your heart and ears tuned to His voice. This daily "tune-up" will help you hear His directions more easily throughout the day. God told me once: "How can you complain about not having answers when you never take time to come talk to me?" That is an ouchy truth, but it is certainly a reality! Take a moment every morning to talk to God.

Scripture: We cannot hear from God if we do not know what His voice sounds like. Reading the Word of God (the Bible) helps us learn how He thinks, how He talks, and how He walks. It does not matter how much you read! When I first started reading the Bible, I only read ONE SCRIPTURE a day. I eventually worked up to one chapter a day. God just wants to see that you take time to be with Him. Over the course of a month, sometimes I would read an entire book of the Bible. Other times I would hop around and read scriptures that were connected to an issue with which I was struggling. Sometimes I felt like reading the famous stories like *David and Goliath, Jonah and the Whale,* or *Noah and The Ark.* In other seasons I would read about the fierce chicks of the Bible . . . women like Esther, Deborah, and Ruth! When you read the Bible, make it your own! There are no rules. Ask God to guide you and ask the Holy Spirit to give you understanding. You are never too young to start reading the Word!

God has amazing plans for your life; but, in order to receive them, you must desire His directions. Every day, make it a goal to take out your G.P.S. The more time you spend with Him, the more your spirit will be charged with the energy and faith you need to complete the day's mission. When you make yourself available to God, He can guide you through your day and lead you to the best life possible!

Prayer Starter: Dear Heavenly Father, thank You for being the Captain of my ship, the Pilot of my plane, and the Tour Guide of my life. You are the Ultimate G.P.S! You already know the plans You have for me, so help me to be disciplined enough to come to You every day for instructions. I know that when I take time to chat with You, You will not lead me astray, but You will empower me to live a life of purpose, joy, and power!

3. Sovereign God

PRAYING FOR PROTECTION

Psalm 91:14-16 (ESV) "Because he holds fast to me in love, I will deliver him; I will protect him, because he knows My Name. When he calls to me, I will answer him; I will be with him in trouble; I will rescue him and honor him. With long life I will satisfy him and show him My salvation."

When you honor God with your life, He will move mountains to protect you. I will always remember the very day I learned that lesson—that particular morning I woke up earlier than normal. I needed some extra time to get ready before my sixth grade students came to class, so I got dressed quickly and headed out the door. The sun had not risen yet. The dark sky was still a peaceful black, but I was on a mad dash out the door!

Not only was I hustling to get to work, but I also ran out of coffee at home and was craving my morning cup of brew! As I drove away from my house, "something" nudged me to stop and take a moment to pray. I pulled my car to the side and took a few seconds to talk to God. I felt a special burden that day to thank God for my life, for covering me, and for always sending His angels to protect me. After I said "Amen" I was eagerly on my way, but now I had a sweet peace.

I drove to the neighborhood gas station. I politely greeted the clerk as I sprinted toward the coffee makers. "Oh no!" I thought, "Of all the days, today my favorite coffee blend is gone!" She noticed my disappointment, but assured me that the other available blends would be strong enough and taste just as good. As I headed to the cash register to pay, she gave me a big smile and said: "It's on me! Don't worry about it!" I ecstatically said "Thank you!" and headed back to my car when it hit me: God totally just took up the tab on my coffee!!

__Side note:__ Ladies, God is so sweet and He is a total Gentleman. He knows even your smallest, most trivial needs, and He longingly waits to meet them. Oh, how He loves you! Invite Him in to take care of you today.

The more I thought about God's kindness, the more excited I became until I was just overwhelmed with pure joy, feeling wonderfully special! I did not know I was going to run out of coffee that morning, but God already had a backup plan! A free one at that! Little did I know at the moment, however, that my coffee was not the only thing God had covered that day.

Literally seconds after driving away from the gas station, an ominous black van from the opposing traffic swerved on to my side of the road. I was driving straight and he came to a complete stop in the middle of the street. Just 30 feet away, I was positioned to T-Bone him at 50mph. The driver must have been in shock because he was not budging. He sat there paralyzed in fear as cars aggressively headed toward him. I thought of hitting the brakes, but glancing in my rear view mirror, I realized there were cars coming too fast behind me. If I stopped, they would crash into the back of me. There seemed to be no way out and I had no idea what to do.

All of the sudden, I felt myself slowly tilting my steering wheel to the left, gliding into this small gap that had suddenly opened up right between the stopped car and the oncoming traffic. I made it safely through, but as I pulled further and further away I looked back in the mirror only to see car after car slam into him—oncoming traffic screeched to a stop.

Still to this day, I believe the moment I took to stop, pull over, and pray saved my life. It gave me a chance to acknowledge God, thank Him for my angels, and simply recognize that my life is in His Hands. It allowed me an opportunity to slow down, put things in perspective, and to be grateful. In just those few seconds, I was telling God that I know He is ultimately in control. God loves it when we honor His authority in our life. He loves it when we express our gratitude for the way He protects and covers us. A heart of gratitude is born out of humility that says our life is not our own. **Acts 17:24-25 (NIV) reads: "The God who made the world and everything in it is the Lord of heaven and earth and does not live in temples built by human hands. And He is not served by human hands, as if He needed anything. Rather, He himself gives everyone life and breath and everything else."**

One of the best things you can do is to learn the power of prayer in your life. Had I been just a few seconds earlier, that wreck could have changed or taken my life. It was God who helped me out of that potentially fatal accident. He gave me peace before I even knew I would need it. Had I not prayed, I could have been too panicked to know not to press on the brakes or too frazzled to maneuver my way into the small gap off to the side of the road. Prayer is simply talking to God and building a friendship with the One Who created you. He is sovereign: in complete control of everything and everyone that is connected to you. Who better to take time to acknowledge?

Prayer Starter: Dear Heavenly Father, thank You for Your amazing protection! Thank You for orchestrating my every move, my every step, and for leading me to safety. I am so grateful You keep trouble and chaos out of my life. I ask that You continue to block all that tries to harm me. All that I am and all that I have are Yours. Please cover me in Your mercy and Your grace. Keep me safe and always nudge me to pray. I love You!

4. Fear

SHINING LIGHT ON THE MONSTERS UNDER THE BED

Psalm 34:5 (NIV) "Those who look to him are radiant; their faces are never covered with shame."

When I was little I had this special way of cleaning up my room. It worked like a charm. I knew exactly where everything could go and I would be done in record-breaking time. The location, you ask? The magical space underneath my bed.

Yep! That's right! A shove here . . . a push there . . . and voila! All clean; all done! My mom trusted me, so I doubt she ever figured it out . . . or did she? Hmmmm . . . Anyway, whether or not she found out was the least of my worries. Every night I would have to face my own mess. I was too little to feel guilty and shameful for my "clever" behavior. No way! It was something more horrifying than that. It was this odd tendency that the clothes, toys, and Barbies I had shoved away began to look like monsters in the wee hours of the night. It was dark and those figures were scary. Even if I had to go to the bathroom really bad I would not budge. Instead I thought to myself . . .

"I am not moving! If I get off this mattress, something will grab my ankles, something will touch my leg!" I vowed that I would wait until the sun came up or the lights turned on before I would dare move. There had to be light so I could see that the monsters were not getting me.

The other day it hit me: As we grow up and as life gets tougher, we can still "put monsters under our beds." When we have painful experiences, it seems easier to push things under the rug than to face them. Rather than attempting to hide items in a play box, we often try to hide our true feelings and emotions from God:

sadness from losing a friend . . .

  fear of being rejected or left out . . .

   frustration over being misunderstood . . .

    anger from our past . . .

     shame from hidden sin and heavy secrets . . .

      pain from breakups . . .

       anxiety over not reaching our goals and dreams . . .

      the list can go on . . . and on . . .

Shoved away for too long, we risk letting these areas become "monsters" that paralyze us with a fear to move, to love, to trust, and to dream again. We risk missing out on some of the greatest blessings of life and even fulfilling our purpose when we do not let God into certain places of our heart. Trust me: it may seem comfortable for a while, but it is not worth it in the long run. We must let God in to heal our wounds if we ever want to stop bleeding from the painful times in life.

One of the most powerful things you can do is to trust God with that places that hurt. The experiences that are the most confusing, frustrating, disappointing, and hurtful are best handled in His Hands. Those moments where you might have said: "I'll just get over it," "I'll eventually forget," or, "I'll just move on," are usually the moments you should pray about and revisit with God. Be brave! We do not want to sweep them under the rug or shove them under the bed. It is only when we allow God to shine His light on these areas that we can begin to heal from the pain.

Today, don't be afraid of addressing the monsters under your bed. You don't have to face them alone. Your Mighty God, your precious Heavenly Father, is right there by your side willing to hold your hand and walk you through. He will not rush in and make you feel horrible about your life. He loves you to wholeness. He loves you to freedom. He is a God of Justice and much Grace. I have seen Him help me forgive people I never thought I would ever talk to again. I have seen Him bring peace to my relationships and restore dreams I thought I let slip away. I have felt His love pick me up when I felt covered in sin and shame. Jesus is the ultimate Gentlemen. Will you let Him be *The Son* in your dark places? Will you be courageous and let Him in today?

Prayer Starter: Dear God, give me the courage to face the places I hurt the most. Whether it is in anger or whether it is in tears, help me to boldly come to You, knowing that Your arms are open and Your love never runs dry. Nothing is too scary for You! I know that Your light brings hope, joy, and wholeness! I trust You with our whole heart, knowing that You can handle me and all the monsters under my bed.

5. Angels in Disguise

GOD'S SECRET SERVICE

Psalm 91:11-12 (NIV) "For he will command his angels concerning you to guard you in all your ways; they will lift you up in their hands, so that you will not strike your foot against a stone."

Usually when we think of angels we think of these amazingly tall, brilliantly white, effervescent beings who glide across the sky and proclaim beautiful praises to the God of the heavens. Although the Bible teaches us that the appearance of angels is absolutely magnificent, I believe God also sends many of His angels in disguise.

One of my favorite aspects of attending college in Chicago was riding the city bus. I was a southern girl from Humble, Texas, but I always felt my inner city girl got a chance to come out and play when I explored the dazzling lights and the mesmerizing skyscrapers of "The Chi." I enjoyed navigating the dangers of the urban life, too! I had it all down pat, especially my: *"Don't even think about playing with me!"* face when creepy men tried to look my way. I knew what routes to take, how to safely guard my valuables on the ride, and how to double check my seat for any belongings I may have left behind. Having successfully executed this safety routine for three years, I was pretty confident. But one day I was so in a rush that I threw caution to the wind.

Thirty minutes after I hopped off the bus, I realized I left my phone on the seat. By this time, in the middle of rush hour, at least 50 to 100 people would have already gotten on and off that bus. I frantically scavenged through my backpack hoping my missing phone would magically appear, only to confirm that it was indeed on a cross-city tour of Chicago!

When I finally got a hold of a friend's phone, I used it to call the central bus station! Lo and behold, they found it! Someone, out of the complete kindness and honesty of their heart, had actually found the phone and turned it in to the bus driver!

"Woo hoo! Thank You, Jesus!" I thought. They gave me the directions and I happily headed to the station. As I sat on the bus watching the city go by in a blur, I began to notice the scene was changing. The buildings were becoming more rundown, the lawns were not as nicely groomed, and the skyscrapers that once mesmerized me were becoming a lot smaller and more distant. With every stop, there were less and less people on the bus with me. We were headed out of the city to a neighborhood I had never been to before and the people on the bus seemed to recognize that as they stared at me like I was a lost child.

I nervously tried to avoid eye contact because I no longer had the guts to throw the hard eyes like I did to those creepy men in the city. As the bus rolled up to my stop, I hastily got off, only to be greeted by a man openly pulling out his gun on the street corner. He looked at me, and without even thinking I put my head down. I did not say a word and began booking it to the bus station I saw a half mile up the street. I have never walked that fast in my life! All I knew was there was about to be trouble and I had to get out of there. I picked up my phone from the "lost and found" department and headed back to the bus praying the whole way.

"God, please cover me. Please keep me safe! Please!" I prayed . . . desperately trying to fight back tears of utter fear. I wanted to kick myself for not bringing a friend along with me and for not telling my family where I went. My bus came right away so, luckily, I did not have to wait on the corner too long.

Trying to avoid eye contact with the other passengers, I quickly found a seat; but, the smile of this older lady sitting in front of me kept drawing my attention. She looked at me and asked where I was going. She said she could tell I was not from around there and that I needed to be safe in that area. I will never forget her name: Ollie White. How fitting for a lady I would soon realize was an absolute angel (minus the white wings)!

That day Ollie and I spent the next hour chatting. She told me all about her son who was my age. She said that if he ever moved to a new city that she would never want him roaming around by himself not knowing where he was going. An hour flew by as she told me a little about her life and shared a few tidbits about the city I used to think I was good at exploring. People did not bother me when they saw Ms. Ollie by my side. I felt so safe in her presence. She made me feel at peace, almost as if I had found a long lost grandmother. Before I got off at the bus stop near my college campus, I asked Ollie where she was headed. She said, "Oh now, child, I am going back." What I realized then was that Ms. Ollie was supposed to get off the bus close to where I had gotten on. She rode the bus an extra hour out of her way! We passed by her stop a long time before, but my angel in disguise was determined to get me back to campus safely.

A year after I graduated, I went back to Chicago and remembered Ms. Ollie. I managed to successfully research where she worked. This time (with my older sister driving me) I surprised her at her job at the *Field Museum* with chocolates and flowers—a small token of appreciation for a true angel in disguise.

Prayer Starter: Dear Heavenly Father, thank You for all the ways You cover me without me even knowing. Thank You that today and every day, You dispatch Your angels in concern of me. I appreciate both the heavenly angels who watch over me and the people You strategically bring into my life that simply guide me along. I pray for wisdom to stay on Your protected path for me, but I also thank You in advance for Your abundant mercy when I stray. You are one amazing Father!

6. BAE's & BFF's

KEEPING GOD FIRST PLACE IN YOUR LIFE

John 15:13 (ESV) "Greater love has no one than this, that someone lay down his life for his friends."

What's today's lesson? Depend on God for pretty much . . . everything.

As you grow up, you begin to realize that He is literally the only person who will have your back 100% of the time. Even family members, best friends, boyfriends, teachers, and mentors fall short at times. Just like you, they are only human and they were never created to fulfill your every need. In fact, when you approach your relationships with the expectation that people can complete you in any way, you will find yourself sorely and continually disappointed. Learn to save yourself the heartache now!

I did not realize I was so people-dependent until I hit college. In high school I had a few good friends, but it was not until I stepped onto the University of Chicago campus that I found people who felt like long lost brothers and sisters. They had the same quirky personality, odd humor, and rare interests. They possessed a pizzazz for life, but were still driven and ambitious. It was an exciting time and one in which I felt at home. I would soon learn, however, that if I did not balance my excitement for my new friends, this blessing could become a curse.

As I grew closer to my friends, I became comfortable discussing the problems I had in life. I was either on the phone whining or pulling them into a coffee shop for an impromptu counseling session. As they desperately tried to console me, I would usually tell them about how another friend let me down. The more I shared with them, the more dependent I became. Eventually, I started to get nervous about making them upset. I wanted to do anything to avoid conflict because I did not want to lose a friend. What was the result, you ask? I was an emotional mess. As I write this it sounds so pathetic, but back then my feelings were heavy, real, and now I can see that they were unhealthy.

One day as I reached for the phone to call a friend for another "pity me" session, I heard God gently say: "Why don't you talk to me instead?" Although it was a nice request, at first, my pride grumbled in protest at first. I soon calmed down and obeyed.

That was the day I learned that God wanted me to come to Him first. My identity was too wrapped up in being accepted and approved by others. I got so caught up in maintaining my earthly friendships that I forgot about the most important one! My relationship with God! He did not want to be stuck in a Sunday box; He wanted to be a part of my everyday life. Although my friends were wise, He is the Giver of Wisdom. Who could counsel me better? Rather than running to people, I learned to run to God.

I found out that I could trust Him and talk to Him about EVERYTHING!
Nothing is off-limits!

God is and will always be "all ears." I knew He would never roll His eyes and walk away out of annoyance or frustration. I did not have to fret over my private conversations turning into rumors or gossip. I did not have to experience the struggles of taking the wrong advice. Even better, my relationships with my friends grew stronger because they were free of the extra burdens and pressure I unknowingly placed on them.

Today I challenge you to reflect on your friendship with God. He is the real "Before Anyone Else." He is the real "Best Friend Forever." God did not create us to be people-dependent; He created us to be Jesus-dependent. He has given us friendships and community to lean on when we need it, but He never wants us to place people higher than Himself. God is the source of all life, the Creator of the universe. What more do we need that cannot be found in our Friend Jesus?

Prayer Starter: Dear Heavenly Father, remind me that You are first every day! I thank You for the friends in my life, but I pray that I will always lean on You more than people. You are my priority! I know I can talk to You about any and everything. I love that You will always have my back. Help me create healthy, vibrant, and strong friendships that draw me closer to Your Heart. Thank You!

7. Owning Your Uniqueness

DARE TO BE DIFFERENT

I Peter 2:9 (AKJV) "But you are a chosen generation, a royal priesthood, an holy nation, a peculiar people; that you should show forth the praises of him who has called you out of darkness into his marvelous light . . . "

L iterally my entire life I have been called "weird." From elementary school to college and even now into my young adult life people have found me strange. It still amazes me that although I switched schools and moved states several times growing up, this label would follow me no matter the setting. I would put up a front and pretend that it did not bother me, but deep down inside it was truly hurtful. It confused me. It would be one thing if I went out of my way to stand out, but that was never my intention. I could not for the life of me understand what made me so different and why people felt compelled to tell me.

It was not until two years ago (at the age of 24), when I ran across this scripture (I Peter 2:9), that I began to embrace this "weirdness." When I read it, tears started streaming down my face. The word PECULIAR jumped off the page and pierced my hardened heart.

In that moment I began to thank God that I was different. I realized that what people found odd had often related to my love for God and the result that the reality of His love had on the decisions I made in life. I was found weird because I hung out with people who were not in the "in crowd." I was found odd because I did not drink in college. I was found strange because I desired to wait for marriage and not sleep around. People looked at me funny because I enjoyed going to church. They laughed at me because I did not curse. They giggled when I showed interest in school. They mocked me because I desired to do what was right even when it would have been less socially painful to go along with what was wrong.

Indeed I was "weird" and now I thank God that I was truly <u>peculiar!</u>

I Peter 2:9 says we are "CHOSEN," "ROYAL," and "HOLY." Other translations describe us as an "ELECT race," an "ACQUIRED people of KINGLY lineage." Some Bible versions say that we are "people belonging specially to God" and "for God's own possession." All of these adjectives and adverbs connect to being uniquely set apart for God and purposefully selected for greatness.

God was saying to me: "Stop trying to blend in when I have made you a standout!

We were created for God's glory. The way that we are called to live on this earth will set us apart from the crowd and make us distinct from the pack. We are not average women called to an ordinary existence. We were uniquely created to bring glory to God in ways no other human can. How dare we try to be normal?!

Living for God can be tough because it requires us to often go against the grain of modern culture. However, be encouraged today that when you sacrifice what is pleasurable now, God will always honor you later. It amazes me that many folks who teased and singled me out have reached out to me for prayer or advice in my adult life. As they grow up they see more clearly the consequences of peer pressure and the results of succumbing to societal norms at a young age. In moments like these I do not let pride puff me up; but rather, I thank God for preserving me. I thank Him for giving me the strength to endure many sleepless nights with tear-soaked pillows when I had no idea if I would ever fit in or find people who understood me. I thank Him for helping me push through my insecurities and social anxiety to finally reach a point where I am comfortable in my own skin. I thank Him for helping me own my "weirdness" and recognize that it was only by His grace that I am where I am today.

Have you ever felt "weird" or misunderstood? Do you ever feel like you never belong or fit in? The results of daring to be different when I was younger have placed me in a position to be more successful and healthy as an adult today. God has set you apart to bring glory to Him like nobody else can. Don't shy away from Him. Take some time to reflect on how you feel in your own skin. Be honest with God about what challenges you have when it comes to going against what is popular and resisting peer pressure. Ask Him to strengthen you today, so you can be an even more amazing woman tomorrow.

Prayer Starter: *Dear Heavenly Father, how amazing You are! Empower me today with the grace to own what makes me unique and different. Help me to live boldly for You and grant me the strength to make decisions I will be proud of later. I want to shine for Your glory! Help me to walk out my journey in Christ with confidence and flair! I love You!*

Part 2

HEART CONDITIONS:
Checking Your Character

Sometimes we get so focused on presenting a pretty outside, that we forget to care for the inside. God is not fooled by our presentation though. He is concerned about our hearts. Whether its behind closed doors or front and center on stage, everything about our life should reflect the character of Christ. As you work through this second section, I challenge you to truthfully answer this question: Are your thoughts and the desires of your heart pleasing to God? When we are truly living for Him, we won't have to shout it from the mountaintops. When Jesus is really tattooed on our hearts, He will most clearly be seen in our character. It is our job to allow God to help us align our attitude, our mindset, and our beliefs with His. Let's invite God to strengthen our character.

8. Who's in Your Squad?

CHOOSING FRIENDS WISELY

Proverbs 13:20 (The Message) "Become wise by walking with the wise; hang out with fools and watch your life fall to pieces."

When you are doing life for Christ, community is everything. The Christian journey is one that was never meant to be walked alone. Building community involves getting plugged into a church family and being led by a pastor, but it also includes choosing the right friends and finding great mentors. When we have these people in place, we will have a stronger walk with God because they create the support we need to keep fighting the good fight of faith!

As you live for Christ, the acronym A.G.E. will help you remember the three types of support you need: Accountability, Growth, and Encouragement!

Accountability: Have you ever been in a great conversation with someone only to walk away and find out later that you had food in between your teeth the entire time? All of a sudden what you thought was an awesome connection with someone, seems questionable as you realize that person was not comfortable telling you the truth. In life, you need "truth tellers!" **Proverbs 27:6 (NIV) says it perfectly: "Wounds from a friend can be trusted, but an enemy multiplies kisses."** In other words, you need friends that are cool with calling you out because they know it will make you better. You want people who will tell you when you are being less than your best, people who want to see you succeed in life. Make sure you receive their feedback. They are the ones that can be trusted, not people who flatter you all the time and tell you that you are perfect. No one is perfect. We all have areas we need to work on and sometimes it takes a good challenge from a trusted friend to inspire us to step it up. Find friends that will keep you accountable!

Growth: In addition to good friends, you want people in your life who can mentor you. Mentors should be people that are older than you, who have experienced more in life, and can wisely speak into the situations you may face. As a female, you want to find an older woman who can guide you through the difficult times in life. Be sure that she is someone who shares your same faith and values. **Proverbs 15:22 (ESV) states: "Without counsel plans fail, but with many advisers they succeed."** Having mentors help keep me from so much unnecessary heartache and pain. They help me recover when I mess up in life. My mentors are women with whom I can be COMPLETELY honest. They do not gossip about me or spread my secrets around; instead, they cover me with love and prayer. They help me keep a healthy outlook on life by offering fresh perspective and insight that allow me to view my situations differently. Like a good friend, a mentor should feel comfortable enough to keep it real with you. They will tell you the truth in love, even if it hurts. It is better to receive correction and wisdom now than to be trapped in what could have been an avoidable, dangerous situation later. Find a good mentor!

Encouragement: As the world turns more and more away from the things that please God, it can seem as if you and I are the only two people trying to do life in Christ. However, according to the Pew Research Center, there are 2.2 billion Christians around the world! Girl, we are not alone! This is why fellowship is key! Get plugged in with other believers, other "fellows," who can encourage and motivate you. We are all going through this tough thing called "life" together and sometimes the best thing we can do is to share a good meal and a good laugh with those who love and relate to us. Sometimes it just takes one person being bold enough to talk about Jesus for you to see that there *are* girls just like you out there. There are ladies you can bond with in your classes, in your neighborhood, on your sports teams and within other extracurricular activities that you may be involved in. You want to find friends that are on the same page as you and doing their best to live for God. These should be people who not only respect your values, but also <u>share</u> them. You do not want to befriend people who question your ways or make fun of your decisions. Having friends who possess the same morals is key. Whether we like it or not, it is inevitable: we become like those we hang around.

When it comes to building a healthy community, you must do it prayerfully. Ask God to help you find your friends. Ask Him to highlight a woman in your life that could be a good mentor. Asking your parents or loved ones their opinion is helpful as well. They can usually recognize good and bad characteristics in people when we cannot see them clearly ourselves.

Remember the acronym A.G.E? It is often said that "Wisdom only comes with age," but having good friends and mentors can help us attain that knowledge a lot quicker. Christian community is an invaluable part of your walk with God. Get plugged in and see the benefits it will have on your life!

<u>Prayer Starter</u>: Dear Heavenly Father, thank You for the gift of community! I desire to surround myself with the right people who can motivate me to become my best self. Guide me to the right friends and lead me to the best mentors who can do life with me! I recognize that I cannot do my Christian walk alone. I need You and I need good people.

9. Find Your Stride

RUNNING YOUR RACE AT YOUR GOD-GIVEN PACE

Proverbs 4:25-27 (ESV) "Let your eyes look directly forward, and your gaze be straight before you. Ponder the path of your feet; then all your ways will be sure. Do not swerve to the right or to the left; turn your foot away from evil."

I will never forget my morning jog on July 4th, 2016. I had it all planned out. I normally ran three miles as I worked on getting my heart back into tip-top shape, but this particular day I decided to challenge myself by doing four miles. I was focused on my goal of slowly building my endurance and that day was the day I would push myself an extra mile.

I started on the running trail and reached the first half-mile mark when I spotted her. A blond chick, with a gray shirt, and black shorts was just up ahead of me, about a fourth of a mile. I could see she was in her running groove. With her headphones in, she was cruising at a challenging pace and enjoying a hard run as her gray shirt turned to dark gray, drenched in all her sweat. Then, all of a sudden, every ounce of my competitiveness began to rise up: "I'm going to totally catch her!!" I thought. I did not even give the Holy Spirit a chance to check my pride before I started aggressively increasing my pace. Every few yards, I would speed up. Although I could feel my heart beating faster and my mind telling me to slow down, my flesh wanted the glory of passing her up and letting her know "Hey, I can run too! See, look at me!"

As I inched closer and closer, I knew I could not let her see me gasping for air, so I forced myself to play it cool. Trying to keep my swag and pride intact, I pretended to enjoy my music as I jogged casually by her. It took so much extra energy! Once I passed her, I realized I had taken on more of a commitment than I had planned because now I had to keep the pace; I could not bear the humiliation of her catching up with me!!

So I ran and ran, harder and harder, to create space between me and my "opponent" who at this point could probably care less about what I was doing. I finished the first mile utterly exhausted. Normally I would take two minutes or so to catch my breath, but I was so gassed I needed more time to recover. When my energy finally returned, I headed back to the trail.

Luckily the blond headed off to another part of the course, but half way into mile two, I spotted a brunette in a lime green shirt and leggings. As you can probably guess, I didn't learn my lesson. The urge to compete rose up in me again! Off I went, faster and faster. I passed her up and once again my pride forced me to amp up the pace. I ended the second mile utterly exhausted and could barely finish the third one. Forget my goal of completing four miles! Psshhh! That was out the window! I was so busy trying to keep up with those girls that I was not productive or effective in reaching my own goal.

God has given each of us unique assignments and unique purposes. Life will consistently present numerous opportunities for us to get sidetracked and attempt to run somebody else's race at someone else's pace. However, we must stand firm in what God is calling us to do. We must move when only He tells us to move and at the pace that He has ordained for us to run. Otherwise, we risk not finishing the tasks He has put before us to achieve. We risk wasting time recovering from exhausting activities He never told us to take on in the first place. We risk even suffering injuries to our self-esteem, relationships, and goals because we are running down paths He never told us to explore.

The focus scripture for this chapter says to not swerve and to keep our feet from evil. Some examples of evil are: jealousy, pride, comparison, and competitiveness—these can drive us away from our unique purpose. I say to you this day: *surrender the temptation to taste of these evils in your life!* Be determined to stay your course! Be determined to run your race at your God-given pace!

Prayer Starter: Dear Father God, You are in charge. Help me to relax and simply follow Your lead. There are so many temptations to look to my right and to my left, but I know deep down that I am most successful when I am doing what You have equipped and called me to do. I am not effective when I am trying to imitate or compete with the calling of others. When everyone else seems to be thriving and blossoming, give me the grace to stare straight ahead and keep my eyes fixed on You and Your unique path for me.

10. Gossip

DEATH & LIFE ARE IN THE TONGUE

Proverbs 18:21 (ESV) "Death and life are in the power of the tongue, and those who love it will eat its fruits."

Have you ever caught someone talking negatively about you? Have you ever been caught saying mean things about someone else? It is amazing how just one simple whisper from a friend can completely change your perspective about somebody. Sometimes it is done maliciously as a person intentionally puts another down. Other times it can be an insult disguised as a "harmless" joke. However, every time negative talk is in the air, it threatens to taint what is beautiful.

I can still remember the day I sulked while heading back to my college dorm room after playing horribly at a volleyball tournament. It had been a very long weekend with back-to-back matches and we had just returned from a long road trip with all fifteen teammates cramped together on a tour bus. The ride back was extremely uncomfortable, but what I found even more confining than the limited space, was the overwhelming thoughts of defeat that were crowding into my mind. "You'll never be able to recover from this tournament! Your stats are only going down from here! You let your teammates down! Everybody is disappointed in you! Coach will never trust you to play under pressure again! The way you performed at this tournament was downright embarrassing!"

The thoughts went on and on and all I wanted was a chance to throw myself on my bed, pray, cry myself to sleep, and hopefully wake up feeling better. When I finally made it to my dorm room, I came back out into the hallway to grab my duffle bag only to overhear two of my teammates gossiping about how badly I had played. They were laughing hysterically at my stats and the more they went on, the smaller I felt.

The next few days they acted as if nothing happened. They cheered me on during practice and clapped for me during games, but the foundation of my trust for them was broken. I grew more and more insecure inside, feeling I had no one to truly confide in and no one to genuinely have my back if I failed. Though they smiled at me, all I could hear inside my head were their negative words on repeat. Though I was part of a big team, I felt completely alone.

Proverbs 18:21 (ESV) says: "Death and life are in the power of the tongue . . . " Just by the simple gossip of my teammates, death came to my confidence and to the unity and success of our team. What is even sadder is that those girls always seemed to be on edge, wondering if I had overheard them. As I reflect on the situation, I now recognize how the enemy was working the entire time. He was planting seeds of strife, using words that would not only affect our play on the court, but also our friendship off the court. His ultimate goal was to create an environment of distrust and discord—one in which I would never feel safe sharing my life with them, let alone my faith. That is precisely what the enemy wanted.

God has called us to live in unity, but unity cannot live where there is no trust. Trust is built between people when you know that they are the same in front of you as they are behind your back. When we are caught gossiping, we can either admit we were wrong or pretend like nothing happened. But either way, the bond has compromised. You know the saying: "Forgive, but don't forget!" Even if we want to forget what was said about us, we often continue to hold on to the pain. No matter what we say, words do hurt. Words can create a lifetime of wounds that distance us from receiving and giving love to people, one of the very reasons why God created us in the first place. As strong women of God, let us be determined to breathe life into all we speak with and about today.

Prayer Starter: Dear Heavenly Father, right now I devote my words to You. I know that what I say matters and what I say has power. Father, help me to bring glory to Your Name and to honor all of Your children with the words that come out of my mouth. I desire to be a woman that uplifts and encourages others. When I am tempted to gossip, help me surrender that desire to You. When I am tempted to listen in on the negative conversations of others, give me the strength and wisdom to walk away. I want to be a part of bringing life and light to this world, so help me to speak words of love and kindness.

11. Coveting

LETTING GO & LETTING GOD

Matthew 6:33 (ISV) "But first be concerned about God's kingdom and his righteousness, and all of these things will be provided for you as well."

The Word of the Day is: "Covet." To covet means "to want, to crave, to yearn for, to wish for, to desire, to set one's heart on, to hunger for, and to thirst after." When you covet something, it becomes everything you focus on and think about. You want it so badly that it becomes a burden and it steals your joy when that desire is not fulfilled.

Just like God knows the desires of your heart, the enemy has studied your habits and tendencies as well. He is not able to look into your heart or read your mind like God does, but he takes notes on where you have struggled in the past, what you are easily tempted by, and the things you desire to have in the future. So that you can protect your relationship with God, it is incredibly important to be aware of what consumes your focus and what consistently grabs your attention.

I have noticed that it is during the times when I am the most passionate and focused on God, that the enemy presents his most sneaky threat to my devotion: a temptation to have what I am coveting! Depending on who you are and what you like, you may covet different things: guys, friends, money, popularity, clothes, cars, achievement, a certain body type, a special talent, attention, intimacy, freedom, power, beauty, and fame. The list goes on and on— it is endless.

Just as the enemy gets sneakier with finding new ways to tempt you, you have to get wiser with creating new ways to protect your heart. Our adversary will use any and everything to get us distracted from living the wonderful life Jesus died for us to have; so, we have to be on guard. We will become stronger against his attacks when we become aware of the desires in our heart. Even if we cannot share what we really want with family or friends, we have to get real about it with God. He knows what we hope for and He is the only one that can truly fulfill our longings.

It can be really, really, *reeeaaallly* hard to let go of something you want, but when you trust that God has your best in mind, it gets easier. He will always give you what you need when you need it. If we covet anything, it should be God! When you focus on God, you will see that His timing is perfect and His plans are way cooler and way better than anything you can come up with. He may not always ask you to completely give up something, but He never wants anything to take over your mind and heart more than He does.

If we hunger and thirst after anyone, it should be God. In this season and in every season, be determined to make your relationship with God your number one priority. Be devoted to becoming your best self. Be committed to completing the tasks that God He sets before you. Get fierce about staying focused!

Other versions of Matthew 6:33 say to "pursue" or "seek first the Kingdom of God and His righteousness." My question for you is: what are you seeking and pursuing? Who or what are you coveting? What do you really hope to have, to become, and to do in life? Has pursuing these things become a distraction? If so, bring it before God.

Today, set aside some time to reflect on the list in paragraph three and be open and honest with God about anything that is stealing your focus. Lay it on the altar. He will always do His best to protect you, but you have to first surrender your wants and will to Him.

Prayer Starter: Dear Heavenly Father, this is so hard!! Show me what I am clinging to more than You and help me to let go! I want nothing else and no one else to consume my heart and mind but You. Fill me up and make me whole, so that I do not look to the world and to people to fulfill my needs. Help me seek You, Your character, and Your purpose for my life above anything else that has become a distraction.

12. Jealousy

ISN'T GOD BIG ENOUGH?

Proverbs 14:30 (NLT) "A peaceful heart leads to a healthy body; jealousy is like cancer in the bones."

Have you ever seen a commercial that directly targets and puts down another company's product? Every time I see that it has the opposite effect on me! Instead of agreeing with the advertisement, it makes me realize that the other company must be really good! I think to myself: "Hmmm...maybe I should check them out!" I am sure that is not the reaction that the commercial maker wants, but to me it is logical. Think about it: Companies would not spend millions of dollars to create an ad about a business that was not competition. If they are investing time, energy, and money into ruining the reputation of another product, they must really feel threatened!

Just like companies fight for customers, sometimes we can feel like we have to fight for recognition or put others down so that we look good. It is so easy to fear that the gifts and talents of someone else will outshine ours. If we are not careful to guard our hearts and our minds from this kind of pride and fear, we can waste a lot of time and energy feeling threatened by the success or skills of another person. I have definitely been guilty of this!

When I first started teaching, there was a co-worker of mine who was such a great chick—she had everything together! The school staff loved her! She was not only super-confident and a natural social butterfly, but she was also bilingual and could speak to everybody with spunk and charisma. She was always extremely organized, arrived to work early before anyone else, and stayed late to help the kids improve in reading. She was the model teacher and kept the rest of us rookie teachers working hard and on our toes to keep up. Oh, and did I mention that she was athletic and could outplay the middle school boys on the soccer field!

I admired her so much, but I was also very jealous. I was by no means a morning person, so waking up bright and early to greet 100 hyper sixth graders was a challenge. I took Spanish classes for six years, but had never studied abroad and was too insecure to risk speaking the language in public. Organization was definitely not my strength either. I lived in the art of *organized chaos* in which I declared: "Yes, my desk is junky, but I know *exactly* where everything is!"

The more I had to work with her, the more I felt my weaknesses were dancing in her spotlight for everyone to see. I was not only feeling inadequate to do my new job, but I was also insecure about the fact that I could not enjoy this new friendship because I lacked self-confidence. I was a mess! This wonderful girl was simply living her life and doing her best, and yet it was making me sick to my stomach! I knew then that I had to make a decision.

For weeks I prayed that God would heal my heart and renew my mind. I prayed that He would build my confidence. I asked that He would help me to improve upon my weaknesses and show me my own strengths. At the same time, I prayed that He would protect my friendship with her because I knew that I was in the wrong. I needed grace to keep talking to her and to not turn away in self-pity or start hateful gossip, birthed out of my own sense of defeat. It took time, but God answered my prayer. He helped me to see that I could choose to learn from her and be inspired to get better rather than waste my energy secretly hoping that she would fail. It was not an easy process, but with

God all things are possible—He gave me the strength. If you struggle like I did, He will strengthen you too!

Looking back, what amazes me most is that I would have missed out on one of the most valuable friendships of my young adult life! Believe it or not, this girl has become one of my best friends! We are both very driven women, so for the last few years we have kept each other motivated, accountable, and encouraged as we chase our dreams. We have each gone on to have successful careers where we *both* shine! In fact, I can shine brighter where I am now because of what I learned from her then. It is hard to find true gems like my friend who can celebrate another person's success without being intimidated by it! I would have missed out on a major blessing if I had given into jealousy, insecurity, and fear!

Just like companies only target businesses that are a threat, the enemy targets relationships that are a threat to his agenda. His goal is to create strife and disorder, hatred and discord. He would rather keep us jealous and bitter, but God knows we are better together. Everywhere we go, we will always meet people who are good at something that we do and maybe even better. I have found that every time I decide to surrender my jealousy to God, there is always something amazing on the other side! There is always light at the end of the tunnel! Every time I push through my insecurity God makes me spiritually better, opens up new opportunities, helps me find new strengths, and even new friendships. If you are tempted to fall into jealousy, be determined to push through it and remember that His stage is big enough for all of us to shine.

Prayer Starter: God, this is really hard, but I boldly declare that I will not operate in jealousy! Help me to live at peace with myself and others. When I am tempted to be intimidated by the great qualities of other people, give me the courage to release my feelings and emotions to You. Grant me the grace to celebrate their gifts and give me the wisdom to recognize how beautifully You have created me as well. I trust that what You have for me is for me. Your great God-stage is big enough for everyone and I know that with You I am never lacking!

13. Gratitude

A QUIET & LETHAL WEAPON

Psalm 100:4 (NIV) "Enter his gates with thanksgiving and his courts with praise; give thanks to him and praise his name."

G ratitude is one seriously fierce secret weapon that I just recently discovered. We all grow up learning to say the two magic words: "please" and "thank you." If you are like me, your parents drilled these words into your brain and always made sure you packed your manners when you left the house for the day. However, developing a lifestyle of gratitude takes this to a whole new level. If you grab a hold of this habit, you better get ready for some serious joy and ridiculous power. You have been warned!

For my 25th birthday, my sister bought me a cute, orange, mini gratitude journal. A gratitude journal has become very popular so now they are all super cute and fashionable, but the concept is still simple. Grab a notebook and start capturing the small and big blessings of your day. What you are thankful for may be different each day, but the idea is to start becoming aware of how God is working in your life.

I would always wait until right before I went to bed to pull my journal out and start writing. It was relaxing and one of the best ways to fall into a pleasant sleep. Some days I would write about someone who complimented my smile, getting a free cup of Starbucks coffee, or having a great conversation with a friend. Other days, what I wrote about was more deep and spiritual like getting the opportunity to encourage and minister to someone at church, having the strength to push through a lot of fear or temptation, or seeing a dream come to pass that I had been waiting on for a really long time. When I first started journaling all the things, people, and events that I was thankful for, I only had about three notes on a page. Now I can journal until I completely lose track of time.

Not long ago, in the span of just one week, I closed my thumb in the trunk of my car, two days later my car died after the battery exploded, and the next day I had to take an emergency trip to the hospital for a random health concern. Everything that was happening was not only inconvenient and painful, but also really expensive! It was in the hospital that I began to feel tears well up in my eyes. I knew right then that I had a decision to make. I could either sink into a puddle of self-pity or I could put my big-girl pants on and start thanking God for all the ways He was providing . . . even in the midst of such an unfortunate week.

Right then and there, as I waited to see the doctor, I whipped out my mini, orange journal and went to work! I began to thank God that even though my thumb was caught in the trunk, He kept it from closing all the way and breaking the bone. I told God that even though my car battery exploded, I was grateful that I had successfully reached 100,000 miles in four years without having one wreck or any other big car issues. I finished off by telling Him how much I appreciated that even though the health concern was unexpected and unplanned, I could afford to pay for the visit and the medicine that I needed. These were all tremendous blessings that I did not want to overlook.

Within 48 hours, God turned every last battle around. The numb feeling in my thumb began to dissipate—that saved me almost $150 worth of hospital x-rays! The car repairs that were supposed to cost $190, ended up costing me $20. The unexpected doctor's visit that was estimated at $140, ended up being completely FREE! I should have been broke, without a car, and walking around with a cast on my thumb . . . but GOD!!! WOOOO HOOO! GO JESUS!!!

Thankfulness is not only a lethal weapon against the enemy and his attacks, but it also has some amazing side effects! The more grateful you are, the more joy and peace you will feel. Gratitude helps you release anxiety and gain perspective so that you can become more content where you are on the way to wherever God is taking you. It makes your heart happy when you stop and acknowledge all the little ways He "smiles" or "winks" at you by doing something in your day that is special and unique to you. It can almost leave you breathless to know that the God of the universe cares about every detail of your life. You will see that He has a great sense of humor, that He knows you very well, and that His timing is always perfect when it comes to answering your prayers. Thankfulness is a lethal weapon against the enemy. Start wielding it in your life!

As you begin to thank God for all the tiny and awesome blessings of your day, just wait and see what He will begin to do for you. God loves it when His people have hearts of gratitude and go throughout their day expectant for what He can and is longing to do! God wants to bless you!

Prayer Starter: Dear Heavenly Father, YOU ROCK! There is no other God like you. Thank You for blessing me with a heart of gratitude. Open my eyes to see the little things You do to take care of me and remind me to be grateful for the big battles You help me overcome. You are God of it all and for this I am thankful!

14. Input Output

WHAT GOES IN MUST COME OUT

Galatians 6:7-8 (ESV) "Do not be deceived: God is not mocked, for whatever one sows, that will he also reap. For the one who sows to his own flesh will from the flesh reap corruption, but the one who sows to the Spirit will from the Spirit reap eternal life."

W hat's been coming out of your mouth lately? What kind of thoughts do you typically have in the course of a day? Imagine that someone was recording everything running through your mind. Would you be okay with them watching and listening in? Or, are there some parts you would rather they hurry up and fast forward? Your response to these questions matter. Your thoughts not only influence your success in life, but they also greatly affect your walk with God.

Where do your thoughts come from? Well, a lot of times what we watch, read, and listen to influences what we think, feel, and say. Have you ever noticed if you hang around your best friend for too long you begin to start acting like them? You start using the same phrases and can even tell what each other is thinking. It is the same way with television shows, books, magazines, video games, social media, and especially music! We have to be careful about what we take in because it will surely come out!

The summer before I began playing college volleyball, I was up early running or lifting weights every morning. For me, nothing was better than working out and listening to music. I turned it all the way up!! As the music pumped into my ears, I was motivated to keep going. I started out listening to Christian music, but eventually I got bored. It did not have the bass and the excitement I enjoyed in secular music. I missed that cool feeling, so I began searching online for some of the top hits. This music had amazing bass and provocative beats, but along with that came one curse word after another. I convinced myself that I could listen to this music without it impacting me, but boy I was wrong! As I pictured the lyrics, seductive images bombarded my mind. The music felt good to listen to, but it was as if the lyrics were cutting my soul.

By the time I got to campus, I noticed my thoughts were changing. I began to look at the guys differently. I wanted them to think about me like the music artists described the girls in the songs. I craved the attention they got in the music videos and wanted someone to desire me in that way . . . even if it was only for my looks or my body. I knew deep in my spirit that it was wrong, but the lyrics made it seem so glorious to have all the guys' attention. The music videos painted the picture that it was something every woman should want and desire.

Eventually, what I was thinking began affecting how I acted. I started carrying myself differently. I flirted with guys in the gym and dressed less modestly when I went out with my friends. Sometimes I even let a curse word slip. My teammates would look at me in shock. They cursed, but they were not used to *me* doing it because I was the "Christian girl"...the "goody two shoes." I knew these moments damaged my reputation, and I now realize how it hurt my witness.

How could I be "the light" on campus if I was walking in such darkness? How could I say I represented Jesus when my actions were declaring something else?

I continued to explore the party life for a while; but, when I hung out with my Christian friends, I felt how empty I was on the inside. I knew that if I did not change what I was listening to, who I was hanging out with, and what I was watching, things were only going to go downhill.

My mother told me once that even if I could not talk to her about something, I could always talk to God. In college I used that advice more than ever. I was too embarrassed and ashamed to tell others, but I knew I could turn to Jesus. I was painfully honest with Him. I asked if He would purify my mind, change the desires of my heart, and help me want the things that pleased Him.

It was not overnight, but as the days went by, I began to blossom in my relationship with God. He helped me build godly friendships and I started losing my craving for the kind of music and behaviors that were only holding me back. During this time, I realized God wanted to help me, but I had a role to play in my transformation. I had to start being disciplined with my input so I could have holy output.

Take some time to honestly reflect on your entertainment and friends today. Sometimes living for God is unpopular, uncomfortable, and it usually goes against the grain of culture, but it is well worth it! Now that I am a young adult, I am grateful that I turned back to Jesus because it allowed God to protect me tremendously. God kept me from making life-changing decisions that would have dishonored Him and my body—choices that could have negatively affected the wonderful plans He had for my life. He protected me from harmful places and people. Of my shame and disgraceful actions, He cleansed me. He gave me opportunities I did not feel worthy of and even lifted me up onto a platform where I can now minister to others.

2 Timothy 2:21 (ESV) says: "Therefore, if anyone cleanses himself from what is dishonorable, he will be a vessel for

honorable use, set apart as holy, useful to the master of the house, ready for every good work." My challenge to you is to learn this while you are young! If you are struggling with being around the wrong people or taking in negative influences, God is always reaching out and giving you an opportunity to change. Will you reach up and grab His hand?

Prayer Starter: Dear Heavenly Father, I want to honor You with the influences I allow into my life. Forgive me for what I have done wrong and give me the strength to do it right. Please help me to desire the things that glorify You and make me a better person. Please send the right friends my way and lead me to the best kind of entertainment. I want to walk in power and I know this starts with guarding what comes into my mind. Give me the grace I need! I know that with You by my side I can do this!

Part 3

DIVINELY ALIGNED:
Walking in Purpose Daily

It is often said that "Your life may be the only Bible someone ever reads." As you move through this third section, I encourage you to reflect on this question: What does your life say about you? As a Daughter of the Most High God, when people see you, they should see Jesus. As a "Jesus Chick" you are called to operate in excellence. How you walk, how you talk, and how you treat others should let them know Who you belong to, what you stand for, and Who you represent. You set the bar high in life. You uphold a mighty standard. You function above the status quo. Let's lean on God to help us walk in purpose daily.

15. The God-Confident Woman

REDEFINING ATTRACTIVENESS

Proverbs 31:30 (NET) "Charm is deceitful and beauty is fleeting, but a woman who fears the Lord will be praised."

In today's world, the "confident" woman is often portrayed as the one who is the loudest, most outgoing, and able to capture any man with her charm. She is locked and loaded with the sharpest of insults to cut down those who dare come against her! The less clothes she wears, the more "glory" she gets because she is "confident" enough to bear it all. She can demand anything and get it at her fingertips. Check the reality shows! Check the Twitter threads! Check the entertainment sites! These "confident" women are everywhere.

They are so present that at times it is easy to second-guess what we should look like, sound like, and strive for in life. Sometimes I think to myself: Is this truly how I have to act to be someone, to get somewhere, or to be recognized in this world?

But today, I offer you a point to the contrary:

There is hope for the <u>God</u>-Confident Woman.

More than just having hope, I truly believe the God-Confident woman is where it is at! She has a presence that commands the room without commandeering it. She is not weak, but she has a quiet swag. She understands that there is no need to shout from the mountaintops because her greatness is written all over her.

*The **<u>grace</u>** of her stride, the **<u>respect</u>**ability of her dress, and the **<u>purity</u>** of her mouth says it all:*

"There is something special and genuinely beautiful about that girl!"

Rather than boasting about herself, her loving spirit, confident humility, and willingness to help others draws people to her. She seeks out opportunities to lift people up, not tear them down. People wait on the edge of their seats to hear what will come out of her mouth because her actions have gained her credibility, respect, and honor. She is a woman of knowledge and wisdom; deceit and gossip are far from her tongue.

She sees no need to clamor for fame. She knows shoving others out of the spotlight is not a necessity. In fact, the spotlight finds her. Favor with God AND man chases her down. She is anointed. She is appointed. She is approved.

Deep in her spirit she knows that all she does, is, and will ever be, is because of her Heavenly Father above. Therefore, this God-Confident woman puts God first and honors Him with her best. She trusts that He will more than supply all of her needs: physically, emotionally, spiritually, financially, and relationally. She believes He has taken care of it all, so . . . she rests confidently in Him.

Today is a great day to take a *God-Confidence Check!* How have you been feeling about yourself lately? Are you ever tempted to compete for attention? Do you sometimes worry that God will not fulfill the desires of your heart and leave you hanging? Do you trust that He can help you achieve your dreams and reach success without compromising your values?

As you honestly reflect on these questions, open up to God and know that He wants to make you whole, secure, and confident in Him. When a woman knows who she is in Christ, there is nothing more beautiful. You will not be tossed to and fro by the fads of this world and your self-esteem will not be shaken by the opinions of others. You will not worry about your future and you will relax knowing that God loves you in spite of your past. Choose to go deeper in your trust with Him today. Choose to be a God-Confident Woman.

Prayer Starter: Dear Heavenly Father, the world has its own idea of beauty, fame, and glory, but I want to be led in the truth and nothing but the truth. Show me what it means to be a God-Confident woman in a world that teaches me that my worth is only skin deep. Help me trust that You have me and my future in the palm of Your Hand. Remind me that I do not have to step on the strides of others to get to the "top." As I seek to honor You through my choices and my character, I trust that You will get me to where I need to be. You know the desires of my heart and I can rest knowing that You will meet my every need.

16. Perfect Timing

SPARING NO GOOD DEED

Matthew 25:34-40 (NIV) "Then the King will say to those on his right, 'Come, you who are blessed by my Father; take your inheritance, the kingdom prepared for you since the creation of the world. For I was hungry and you gave me something to eat, I was thirsty and you gave me something to drink, I was a stranger and you invited me in, I needed clothes and you clothed me, I was sick and you looked after me, I was in prison and you came to visit me.'

"Then the righteous will answer him, 'Lord, when did we see you hungry and feed you, or thirsty and give you something to drink? When did we see you a stranger and invite you in, or needing clothes and clothe you? When did we see you sick or in prison and go to visit you?'

"The King will reply, 'Truly I tell you, whatever you did for one of the least of these brothers and sisters of mine, you did for me."

One day I was grocery shopping at Wal-Mart and I had a particular taste for yogurt. As I reached up to grab one lucky container, eight more came tumbling down from the display. I looked down and was relieved that none of the yogurt had splattered onto the floor, but I was horrified that as I bent down to pick them up, I began losing grip of the other items in my hands. It was as if all my groceries planned to have a surprise party...right there on the floor...in the middle of aisle nine. Utterly embarrassed, I bent my head down quickly in an attempt to deflect everyone's attention from the clumsy scene, but I will always remember what I saw out of the corner of my eye . . .

A young teenage girl and her mother slowly scooted their cart right behind me. I could sense from the slow speed of their cart that they were staring at me and the mess I had made. I could tell that as their wheels glided behind me they were moving with hesitance, as they pondered whether or not to help me. But, the wheels never stopped. The girl and her mother kept going—scooting right along. It seemed as if they had resolved that I should be able to take care of it myself.

The truth is, of course I could take care of it by myself. It was just a few containers and I was simply picking up items off the floor. But . . .

Why not help anyway?

How often do we see people struggling, but we choose to look away? How often do we see people lonely, but we choose not to befriend them? How often do we ask God to help us change the world, but we have not mastered the art of simply lending a hand right in our own neighborhood? **Luke 16:10 (NLT) says: "If you are faithful in little things, you will be faithful in large ones. But if you are dishonest in little things, you won't be honest with greater responsibilities."**

If God cannot trust us to tend to the small deeds, then how can He trust us to conquer big tasks? Never underestimate the power of one "small" act of love, compassion, or kindness. We all want to make a difference in the world and God gives us opportunities to start every single day . . . where we are . . . right now: in our own home, in our community, in our church, in our school, or at our job. It's the little acts of kindness that can start a ripple effect of love and show Jesus to the world. It's the little steps of courage that we take to help when others turn away that can bring real change. Scheduled community service events and youth mission trips are wonderful and we should do them, but we do not always have to wait for the perfect time! God is asking us to be the Light every single day!

If those ladies had stopped for a moment to help, perhaps we would have had a chance to bond. Perhaps we could have shown others in the store, the power of "just doing it," just helping! Perhaps today I would be writing to you bragging about how these two ladies and their small act of kindness changed my world and made my day!

Just start where you are! There is never a better chance to help than right now. Don't wait. Just do it! God cares about the small things and He will reward you.

Prayer Starter: _Dear God, give me the courage to help others when I am hesitant. Give me the boldness to act when others_

simply stare and standby. I want to share the incredible love You have given me with other people. I want to be a world-changer and I recognize that I can start today, even right in my own home. As I go throughout my day, please highlight the opportunities I have to shine Your light by assisting others, loving people, and simply being an encouraging friend. I know I am an ambassador for Christ. I want to bring glory to Your Name. Use me today!

17. Step Up Your God-Game

HAVING A SPIRIT OF EXCELLENCE PART 1

Galatians 6:9 (ESV) "And let us not grow weary of doing good, for in due season we will reap, if we do not give up."

There is one quality that will always get you noticed and set you apart from the pack. That divine quality is: excellence! People with a spirit of excellence are those who strive to do their very best at all times. They operate with a high sense of integrity by giving their all. No matter who is watching, they do what is right even when no one is looking. As powerful women of God, we are called to live with a spirit of excellence, but throughout life I have found that there are a few situations where it is especially tempting NOT to live so powerfully. We will explore them in the next two chapters!

#1 When you do not like the task set before you: It is easy to do what you love because your passion naturally motivates you; but, how do you act when you do not like what you have been asked to do? I never had a problem pushing myself on the volleyball court, but I became a different person when my mother asked me to clean my room or do the laundry. Because I despised cleaning, I would drag my feet, reluctantly head to my room, and find any short cut possible. I pushed things under my bed or into the closet hoping she would not find out. In the end, I was the one left to deal with my own disorganized, stressful, and cluttered room. The truth is, I had "cleaned" my room, but God still had some serious work to do on cleaning my heart. I needed to grow in excellence. In life, we will always have tasks we enjoy and tasks we dislike, but as ladies of excellence, we are called to do them BOTH to the best of our ability!

1 Corinthians 15:58 (NLT) encourages us: "So, my dear brothers and sisters, be strong and immovable. Always work enthusiastically for the Lord, for you know that nothing you do for the Lord is ever useless."

#2 When no one is looking: It s one thing to work hard when an authority figure is watching: a teacher, a coach, a principal, a boss, etc. We love the recognition and attention we receive when others see us hard at work; but, how do you respond when they step out of the room, out of the gym, or out the office? When they leave, do you cut corners and slack off or do you continue to work well and give your best? We must remember that ultimately God is <u>always</u> looking. He is not a mean, overbearing manager, waiting for us to mess up; rather, He is longing for us to prove Him right. He wants our actions and character to match the wonderful things He says about us in His Word. We have to believe that when our life aligns with His principles, we will undoubtedly be blessed. He wants to promote us, but this comes when He first knows He can trust us. Often our truest selves will be seen in the dark, when no one is looking.

Matthew 6:3-4 (ESV) states: "But when you give to the needy, do not let your left hand know what your right hand is doing, so that your giving may be in secret. And your Father who sees in secret will reward you."

If you have big, God-sized dreams for your life, you must have the character to match it. God needs to know that when you make it to the "big leagues" your approval will not come from people. The Bible teaches us not to live for the glory of man, but for the glory of God. He needs to know that you will do the right thing at all times. Having a spirit of excellence will keep you from fumbling the success that comes your way. As you reflect on your level of excellence, be honest with God about where you can do better. He is a gracious God, always looking for the best in us. Live with excellence!

Prayer Starter: Dear Heavenly Father, I desire to be a woman of excellence. I know that You have big things in store for me and I want to be a good steward of all that You have planned. Help me to do the best I can when it comes to taking care of my responsibilities, even the ones I dislike. I want to honor You with my life and exemplify Christ in my character. Build in me a spirit of excellence.

18. Step Up Your God-Game

HAVING A SPIRIT OF EXCELLENCE PART 2

Galatians 6:9 (ESV) "And let us not grow weary of doing good, for in due season we will reap, if we do not give up."

A spirit of excellence is cultivated, not just granted. When something is cultivated it requires time to grow, time to improve, and time to be strengthened. It also involves preparation! I am most successful at living a life of excellence when I prepare my mind in advance. have to make up my mind that I will do and give my best before I enter into difficult and tempting situations.

The following two situations are the ones I have found the most challenging:

#3 When you do not like who you work for: Have you ever been asked to help or work for a person you did not like? That is always a tough situation because it is easy to feel like certain people do not deserve your help or even your respect. You might feel underappreciated or overlooked and you might even have a legitimate reason to feel enraged. Still yet, even in these difficult moments, we have a decision to make. Who are we going to work for: God or people? If we slack off, we are certainly not helping the other person, but we are also not making ourselves look the best either!

At the end of the day, as a Woman of God, you have two brands: you represent Jesus and you represent yourself. Every day you add to that brand or you take away from it. Making the decision to honor God despite how you feel about a person gets easier when you remember that, not only is your reputation at stake, but also your Boss is ultimately God. You work for Him! You work to make Him proud. God honors people who love other people, even when it is hard.

Colossians 3:23-24 (ESV) reminds us: "Whatever you do, work heartily, as for the Lord and not for men, knowing that from the Lord you will receive the inheritance as your reward. You are serving the Lord Christ."

#4 *When you are tired*: When I am tired, I feel like I am absolutely no good to anybody. This usually happens when I am hungry or when I have not gotten enough sleep. I love to help people when I feel upbeat and energetic, but it is incredibly hard to go the extra mile when I do not feel 100%. While it is important to not overextend ourselves by agreeing to help other people when we have not had enough rest, it is equally as important to keep our word and stick to our commitments. If you find yourself in a position where you are tired, but others are still expecting you to fulfill your commitment that is the perfect time to pray for God to give you the strength to deliver on your task. After you have handled that responsibility, then you can plan ahead to avoid being overbooked and overworked next time. God loves to use people who are loyal, faithful, and devoted to their responsibilities! Yet, we also should avoid making empty promises.

Matthew 5:37 (NLT) cautions us: "Just say a simple, 'Yes, I will,' or 'No, I won't.' Anything beyond this is from the evil one."

As we walk out our journey to becoming ladies of excellence, we must be gracious to ourselves! Character is not built overnight; it is built daily. Every single day God is grooming us, growing us, and giving us grace as we strive to become our best. We are always *becoming*. Every morning prepare your mind for excellence and allow God to do the rest. When we continually surrender ourselves to Jesus, He will empower us to be women of excellence.

Prayer Starter: *Dear Heavenly Father, thank You for consistently making me better! In this life, I understand that I represent Jesus and myself and I want to do whatever it takes to represent these brands to the best of my ability. Help me to remember that I am not alone and that every single day You are by my side empowering me to do and to give my best in every situation. I love You. I thank You. I trust You.*

19. God Whispers

LISTENING TO THE STILL SMALL VOICE

John 14:25-27 (ESV) "These things I have spoken to you while I am still with you. But the Helper, the Holy Spirit, whom the Father will send in my name, he will teach you all things and bring to your remembrance all that I have said to you. Peace I leave with you; my peace I give to you. Not as the world gives do I give to you. Let not your hearts be troubled, neither let them be afraid."

Have you ever been in a confusing situation and wish you had someone to turn to for advice? Have you ever been alone and wanted your best friend to show up and give you a big hug? What about the last time you took a tough test or needed to make a difficult decision, could you have used someone to help you through that moment? For Daughters of the Most High King, we have this "someone." This Someone is called: the Holy Spirit.

After spending three years with Jesus, the twelve disciples were frightened when He informed them that He was headed to sacrifice His life on the cross. They responded in fear, denial and frustration! They were not only losing someone that was like a Father and Teacher to them, but someone who was also like a Best Friend! In response to their worries, Jesus replied in **John 14:15-16 (ESV):**

"If you love me, you will keep my commandments. And I will ask the Father, and he will give you another <u>Helper</u>, to be with you forever . . . "

The Holy Spirit is this "Helper". He personally guides us through every waking moment of life. He is not a spooky ghost flying around to creep us out. The Holy Spirit is like a Secret Agent who God assigns to do two main jobs in our lives: PROTECT & EMPOWER.

Having the Holy Spirit is like having Jesus by your side to guide you throughout your day. In life it is often hard to tell what is right or wrong and what is good versus what is great, but the Holy Spirit is the One Who leads us into all truth. He helps us see life more clearly. He assists us in making decisions that please God and He guides us to the best life possible.

The Bible gives the Holy Spirit six different names: The Comforter, The Counselor, The Advocate, The Intercessor, The Strengthener, and The Standby.

#1-2 The Comforter & The Counselor: Life is tough! Growing up my emotions were all over the place as I learned to deal with challenges and frustrations. I often felt sad about not fitting in at school, frustrated over a bad grade, or nervous about a school presentation. For me, discovering the Holy Spirit was life-changing! I learned that when I felt lonely or scared, I could ask the Holy Spirit to <u>comfort</u> me and help me feel better. When I was confused about what to do in a tricky situation, I could ask Him to <u>counsel</u> me and give me advice. Within minutes, I would feel joy or courage starting to rise up inside of me or I would have clarity about a decision I needed to make. You and I never have to stay upset, frightened, or puzzled by life. We can always ask the Holy Spirit to help us!

#3-4 The Advocate & The Intercessor: Many times in life I also needed to be <u>defended</u>! Often I had "haters" at school who would make up rumors or go out of their way to single me out because I was different from them. Fortunately, the Holy Spirit helps here, too! Rather than telling them off after school or being disrespectful, I prayed and asked the Holy Spirit for <u>assistance</u>. I cannot tell you how many times the bully at school would *all of a sudden* leave me alone or even apologize without me having to do a thing! Other times, I simply had desires in my heart that I could not share with anyone and I did not know how to put them into words. As our <u>Intercessor</u>, the Holy Spirit <u>communicates</u> with Jesus about what we are hoping for and longing for in life. As long as we choose to honor God and seek a relationship with Him first, we will see these things come to pass when the time is right (see Matthew 6:33). If we allow Him into our life and ask Him for help, the Holy Spirit will work behind the scenes in ways we could never imagine.

#5-6 The Strengthener & The Standby: The Holy Spirit gives us strength when we are weak and He covers us when we cannot cover ourselves. There will be times when you may not feel like going to school, going to work, studying, or exercising, but the Holy Spirit will strengthen you with the energy you need to complete the task and to do it well! Sometimes we just have to take the first step and get started. He will do the rest! If you are tempted to cheat on a test, to steal, or lie, He can give you the courage to be honest. In other moments, you might be tempted to run off to a secret place with a guy, but deep down inside you know it is a bad decision. Your stomach starts churning and you begin feeling nervous about someone finding out. In these moments, the Holy Spirit is giving you wisdom to walk away and strength to make a better choice. Other times, for example, He will protect you from an accident that should have ended up much worse than it did. In all these situations, the Holy Spirit is your Standby. He works 24 hours a day, 7 days a week, and is always there in cases of emergency, directing you away from trouble and into safety.

The Holy Spirit has many different names, but ultimately He is there to PROTECT & EMPOWER you. Every morning, ask God to help you be sensitive to the leadership of the Holy Spirit. As He guides you throughout the day, be determined to *stop, listen, and obey*. Pay attention to the uneasy feelings you have, the ideas He is trying to give you, and the ways He is making your day easier because you simply asked. If you follow His direction, He will give you favor when you did not earn it. He will bless you with creative ideas and wisdom you could have never come up with on your own. Ultimately, He will lead you to a life of joy, happiness, and health. What more could we ask for?

Prayer Starter: Heavenly Father, thank You for the amazing Holy Spirit who is my Helper! Help me to stop, listen, and obey as He leads me throughout the day. Please tune my mind, ears, and heart to His promptings and warnings. Help me to understand the advice He gives and remind me that I can call on Him for anything and everything. With the Holy Spirit by my side, I am equipped to live a life of greatness.

20. Purity is Power

IT'S WORTH THE WAIT!

Romans 12:1-2 (NLT) " . . . I plead with you to give your bodies to God because of all he has done for you. Let them be a living and holy sacrifice—the kind he will find acceptable. This is truly the way to worship him. Don't copy the behavior and customs of this world, but let God transform you into a new person by changing the way you think. Then you will learn to know God's will for you, which is good and pleasing and perfect."

Waiting for marriage is one of the best decisions I ever made. In fact, I am still waiting and I hope that you will join me. Even if you have compromised, the chance to start again is always available. One of the greatest schemes of the Enemy is to make women feel too used, dirty, and worthless to be any good to God. The truth is, however, that we are never too jacked up for Jesus. At any point, no matter what we have done, He is always offering us forgiveness and a new chance to get on His best path for our life. After reading this chapter, I urge you to prayerfully come to God in this area.

The longer I wait, the happier I get about my choice. Waiting is a decision that will empower you more than you can imagine. A lady sold out for Jesus is downright unstoppable and she will be one of the most powerful women to walk the earth. There is nothing God will not do for a girl after His heart. In God's economy, the deeper we press into Him, the higher He calls us. In other words, God honors those who honor Him. He blesses those, who seek Him. One way that we honor and bless God the most is with our bodies.

Though the media and entertainment industry paint sex outside of marriage as a casual and harmless activity, the nights I have spent consoling my girlfriends have taught me otherwise. SOME of them have been blessed enough to have escaped abusive relationships, unexpected pregnancies, and sexually transmitted diseases, but ALL of them have had to deal with the shame and overwhelming guilt that made them feel distant from God. I have seen the sense of unworthiness, regret, and self-loathing that occurred when a guy they gave their all to walked away like it was nothing.

Trust me: Purity is power. God will not withhold any good thing when you wait on His timing. My friend, it is worth the wait!

Waiting has not been easy, but it has given me time to learn what a good life partner looks like. In college, there were many tempting nights and enticing advances. The guys I dated were all very attractive, smooth talkers, and popular. Being athletic, they were just "my type" . . . or so I thought. Little did I know at the time, I was not "in love," I was "in lust." I admired their physical appearance and paid little attention to their spiritual maturity. Even though these men had faith, we were not on the same page spiritually. I was dumbing down my faith and boldness for God in order to not intimidate them. Although they were successful and driven, their goals in life were not motivated by a mission to bring glory to Christ.

This grieves my spirit to even think about now because I can see more clearly how I was seriously selling myself short. I realize the impact it could have had on the amazing opportunities God has given me as an adult. God wants you to be with someone who can be a good partner-in-purpose, someone who can grow with you on your life journey, someone who truly respects and loves you for more than just your body. God wants to bless you with a guy that loves you like Christ loves the church. That's REAL love worth waiting for! **When you are intimate before marriage, it is more difficult to gauge whether that person is truly God's best for you.**

Waiting to have sex allows me to live life with a powerful level of focus and clarity. Guys are great, but pursuing my purpose wholeheartedly is so much better. When I am crushing on a guy, it gets tough to focus! The more I like him, the more I find myself daydreaming about the next time he will call or text—hoping we can see each other. If we get this consumed emotionally, it only gets more complicated when we add in the physical aspect.

Use your younger years to position yourself for success in your future.

Date your dreams! Date your purpose!

Men will always be there. They are a dime a dozen. It is best to live life focused on what God is calling you to do to fulfill your destiny, to impact this world, and to become a better woman. I have seen too many girls put their lives on hold, move across the country, and even drop out of school to be with a guy. I have seen them shut doors on opportunities that could have bettered their lives. Every time, the guy usually leaves them hanging to pursue another woman. I've learned that what we compromise to keep we will eventually lose. Be wise. Without sex as a distraction, we can make better choices that will affect our future. In the meantime, God is also preparing that special person for you.

Waiting on marriage gives me the ultimate confidence. Nobody can tell me that I am not a catch! My sense of confidence is not based on my appearance or if a guy is pleased with me or not. My confidence is held in the fact that I am fighting the good fight of honoring God with my body. He is empowering me with the grace to fight a tough battle—one that is lost too often in our generation. My self-esteem is found in the fact that God approves of me. When I am married I will be a gift to my husband that no other man has had access to and that puts my heart at peace. I love the idea of being a rare gem, a special and precious treasure.

When I was dating those guys I felt "special" because they "chose" me out of the crop. I felt I was winning! We all like the feeling of victory no matter how shallow the win. But girl, you are a victor in Christ! You do not have to give your body to a man to feel special or approved. God has already chosen you and called you His own.

Do not let the world fool you into thinking confident women give their all to the men in their lives. It takes more confidence, God-Confidence, to say no and wait on God.

Prayer Starter: *Dear Heavenly Father, I know that You will not withhold any good thing from me. I choose to wait until marriage to share my body because I know that I am most powerful when I am 100% devoted to You. As a girl after Your heart, I declare that I will be unstoppable—one of the most powerful women to walk this earth! Give me the strength, the wisdom, and the confidence to fight this good fight of faith. I love YOU!*

21. Esther Influence

CHOSEN FOR SUCH A TIME AS THIS

Esther 4:14 (NIV) "For if you remain silent at this time, relief and deliverance for the Jews will arise from another place, but you and your father's family will perish. And who knows but that you have come to your royal position for such a time as this?"

Often people such as celebrities, governmental leaders, business moguls, and famous athletes are placed on a pedestal. In all their power, influence, and man-made glory, they are idolized and treated as nearly superhuman. As we watch their lives played out on the movie screens, the television, the billboards, and the annual award shows, it can be easy to sit back and assume that God has only called certain people to greatness. We can think: "Those are the 'chosen ones' of society." However, as I have often told my sixth grade students, God did not sprinkle magic fairy dust on a handful of people. When we were born, He did not roam the halls of the hospital contemplating which babies were going to be special and which were not. God has not called any of us to a normal, average, basic existence. God created each and every one of us on purpose and for a purpose; He created YOU for such a time as this!

Every ounce of your being comes together to give God glory like nobody else can (see Colossians 1:16-17). There are unique assignments for you to fulfill, ordained missions for you to accomplish, and special people for you to reach. The enemy's greatest talent is in getting us to think that we are not good enough to be of special value or importance, but I am here to tell you otherwise:

Dear Daughter of the Most High: God needs you. Your entire life is a necessity.

I truly believe each and every single person on this earth is a God-created solution to one of the world's many problems. I believe that your purpose lies in your experiences, your personality, and your gifts. When you submit each of these areas to God, you can then begin to fulfill your potential and walk into your divine destiny. With God, You are unstoppable!

This is why you do not have to look to your left or right and view others as competition. You are not inferior to anybody and you do not have to be intimidated by them. What God has for you is for you. There is territory with your name on it. There are accomplishments waiting for you to achieve. The path He has set before you is uncharted and the shoes He has given you are fitted for your feet. Sure, others can try to fill the void that you will leave if you never step into your purpose, but no one will ever be able to do it like you can. God has fashioned YOU for greatness!

The beauty in all of this is that your destiny is not just about you; your destiny is about everyone attached to you. As you become who God has planned for you to be, you will impact others along the way.

Take Esther for example! Esther, one of the great female heroes of the Bible, had a tough start in life. As a young Jewish girl she lost both of her parents, had to be adopted by her older cousin, and lived as an exile in a foreign nation. When she grew a little older, God ended up positioning her to be chosen as queen of that nation during a time when the Jewish people were being persecuted for their faith. Although Esther was royalty, she doubted her power! She did not know if she truly had the influence necessary to speak to the king, to change the laws that endangered Jews, and to try to save her people. However, God called Esther to do many things afraid. Through a course of miraculous moments in which she courageously stepped out on faith and in obedience, Esther ended up saving the lives of thousands of Jews. When we obey, we gain authority! One woman used her act of obedience to protect countless others!

Side note: The Book of Esther is one of the smallest and most powerful books in the Bible. You MUST read her full story!

Right now, however, I want you to reflect on <u>your</u> story. Think about your uniqueness, your gifts, your personality, and your experiences. Think about what you are passionate about and what problems around the world irk you. Take some time to pray about what God is whispering to you, who He is saying you are, and who He is calling you to be in the future. He can take all of your experiences, the good, the bad, and the ugly and use them for His glory, if you let Him. Even if you think you have the wrong personality for what you want to achieve, trust that God made no mistake when He crafted you. We all are diamonds in the rough, but God will mold us into a work of art.

<u>**Prayer Starter:**</u> ***Dear Heavenly Father, I believe that You have called me to live a dynamic life with a special calling. Help me to see myself as the masterpiece You created me to be. I want to make the most out of my life and impact every person that You have placed in my path. I declare that I matter! I am a woman chosen for such a time as this and I choose to walk boldly and confidently into my future.***

Part 4

GIRL ON A MISSION:
Limitless Living with God

It is easy to live for God when everything is going right, but God wants us to be women who will thrive in every season. He desires for us to lean on Him on the "mountaintops" of life and to trust Him in the "valleys." This is because God uses every single day to prepare us for greatness. Our victories, failures, and disappointments are all a part of walking into our destiny. When we are committed to our faith, there is no stopping us because there is nothing God cannot do with a woman after His own heart. As a "God Girl," when you show up on the scene, it is "game over!" The sky is the limit and nothing is truly impossible when you do life with Him! Your confidence in Christ will not be shaken. You will leave your mark and spark a legacy. My only question for you in this final section is: How would you live your life if you truly believed God was with you and for you? Let's get on with limitless living with Christ!

22. Superwoman

WHAT'S YOUR SECRET POWER?

1 Peter 4:10 (NLT) "God has given each of you a gift from his great variety of spiritual gifts. Use them well to serve one another."

It is time for you to realize that you are downright phenomenal! When God placed you in your mother's womb, He designed you to impact this world like nobody else ever has, can, or will. He equipped you with unique talents and gifts that make you one serious force of nature! Any given day you can spend hours watching people on television cook delicious meals, sing amazing songs, score game-winning points, and decorate everything from cakes to newly bought homes, but God did not create you to just be an observer. God made you to be one stellar and fierce superwoman uniquely designed to operate and function on this earth with power! World-changing, dynamic power!

To be talented is a wonderful thing! Talents are abilities that we can use and experience with our five senses. They typically come in the form of activities like: drawing, writing, painting, singing, dancing, public speaking, playing sports, playing an instrument, acting, etc. When you discover that you have a talent, you should do all you can to develop it and become better at it. The world often celebrates talents because they are easy to identify and fun to put on display for others to enjoy. However, talents are not where our secret powers lie! Our real secret powers are found in our spiritual gifts!

Spiritual gifts are not about being seen or entertaining people. When we use our gifts, they are to positively influence others and bring glory to God. Gifts can change the heart of people, unite divided groups, heal broken souls, and empower others. As you go throughout life, it is should be your mission to discover and develop your gifts. The sooner you realize what they are, the quicker God can use you to impact your friends, your community, and your world.

In my life, God has given me three ways to discover my spiritual gifts:

#1 Discover your gifts by asking questions: Did you know that encouraging people is a gift? How about leading others? How about organizing and planning? What about giving or serving others? Did you ever think that having faith, teaching people, or being able to quickly learn new concepts are gifts? Because gifts come so easily to us, it can be difficult to recognize them. We may not notice that the things we do naturally are actually hard for other people. This is why it is important to take time to reflect on them by asking ourselves and our loved ones meaningful questions: What comes naturally to you? What do people usually compliment you on? What good characteristics or qualities do others notice in you? When you are a part of a group or team, what roles do you normally take on? How do you contribute to the group?

#2 Discover your gifts by looking at the pattern: In elementary school, I was the kid who would go over to the student who was eating by themselves in the cafeteria. While others could go on just fine eating their lunches, I could never seem to enjoy mine until I befriended the one who sat alone. Throughout high school and college, the pattern continued. I became really good at starting random conversations with people and making them feel comfortable with telling me about themselves and their life stories. I never realized this pattern until one day my sister pointed it out. She said everywhere we went I was good at talking to people one-on-one. It turns out that the Bible says this is a gift! It is the gift of hospitality! It is also the gift of encouragement! Today I serve in a position at church where I welcome visitors from all over the world. Every Sunday I meet and greet them by holding mini-conversations to help them feel comfortable and at home. Because they feel at ease with me, many visitors have opened up and asked for prayer. God has used these conversations to allow me to give people hope during tough times. Now I recognize that my gift is about more than just feeling comfortable talking to complete strangers! It is about ministering as well!

#3 Discover your gifts by serving: When you begin to get involved in church, in school, and in your community, God will start highlighting your gifts. You will find that you like certain tasks more than others. Your leaders and the people you help will compliment you on the great qualities you possess and may have never noticed. You will also see what you are <u>not</u> good at and what does <u>not</u> come naturally. That is equally important to note! By getting involved, over time, God will help you discover how He uniquely fashioned you to influence others.

God, the Creator of the universe, made you a force to be reckoned with! In addition to your talents, you have gifts! This week, be bold and ask God to start showing you just how marvelously and purposefully He designed you to operate and function on this earth. The sooner you realize what your gifts are, the quicker God can use you to impact your friends, your community, and your world. We need you, Superwoman! So, get to it!

Prayer Starter: _Dear Heavenly Father, I declare that I am one of a kind! You have designed me to function on this earth like no_ *one else and I want to know more about how You have uniquely created me. Show me what I am good at! Show me how I can influence others for the better. I want to be Your superwoman and positively impact this world.*

23. Hold on to Hope

LEARNING TO DEAL WITH DISAPPOINTMENT

Jeremiah 29:11 (NIV) "For I know the plans I have for you," declares the LORD, "plans to prosper you and not to harm you, plans to give you hope and a future."

J uly 6th, 2014. The feelings I felt on that day were almost unbearable. Stage lights off. The beautiful new Miss Texas whisked away. There I stood, stuffing my bags into the tiny trunk of my car for what was going to be a very long, lonely, and disappointing ride home. All I could think about was the months I had completely poured lots of time, lots of money, and a tremendous amount of effort into a dream that had managed to dissipate right in front of me. My dream of becoming Miss Texas and ultimately Miss America had died and there was nothing I could do about it.

I remember feeling stunned. My emotions were so raw; they were on a roller coaster. I didn't really know how to feel. For months, girls just like me from all around the state ate, slept and breathed the vision of becoming Miss Texas, traveling to speak to thousands of youth around the state! For me, these months were especially a whirlwind because I had never been on the pageant scene before. Because I won my very first local pageant, there was no "test run" or "getting my feet wet." I stepped into my dream quicker than expected and had to work it out and learn on the go. As I prepared for the next level of competition, I found myself completely out of my comfort zone for a complete year. It left me extremely drained physically, emotionally, and spiritually. It was an amazing journey that I would never take back, but it was by no means an easy ride.

On the road trip back home, I was too tired to reach out to anybody. Part of me didn't want to talk . . . not even to God. I went as far as to say out loud: "God, I love You, but I just need some space right now. I do not want to talk."

Some of you are probably reading this and thinking, "BLASPHEMY! How could she say that to God?!" But that is how I honestly felt and exactly what I said. I trusted God would know my heart. Funny thing is, He gave me exactly what I asked for: NOT ONE of my friends reached out to me for an entire week. Come to find out days later, once they all texted or called, each one literally said..."*I wanted to give you space.*" Ha! God has a funny sense of humor, let me tell ya!

At that time though, I didn't find it so funny. Despite what I declared out loud, I did want someone to lean on. God doesn't always give us what we want though. Sometimes He just gives us what we need. Now when I look back at those moments full of pain and drowsy tears, I know I needed that space to remain void. Nothing a friend could have said and not even the best hug from a family member could have filled it. Only God could speak to the hole I had in my heart. Only God could understand the depth of my disappointment.

I look back now and actually thank God for the silence because it was an opportunity to hear His voice. God did not speak to me audibly through some sort of heavenly megaphone saying: "Isis! Here ye! Here ye! Why art thou sad?" But how I explain it is that even in the midst of such great disappointment, I had the strength to pray and ask God for peace and clarity. He began to fine tune my ears to Him and align my heart with His will. He helped me see what I had gained from this experience and how it would propel me into another level of my destiny if I would just trust Him to turn this "loss" into a win. He revealed new visions and stirred up new dreams that excited me even more than the one that died. The minute I began to release my disappointment to Him and made a decision to believe His ways were better than mine, God gave me wisdom. He reminded me to hold on to hope and to remember the promises He gives you and me that are found in the Bible:

- "For I know the plans I have for you," declares the LORD, "plans to prosper you and not to harm you, plans to give you hope and a future" (Jeremiah 29:11 NIV).

- "[H]e will give a crown of beauty for ashes, a joyous blessing instead of mourning, festive praise instead of despair" (Isaiah 61:3 NLT).

- "[W]eeping may endure for a night, but joy *cometh* in the morning" (Psalm 30:5 KJV).

- "And we know that for those who love God all things work together for good, for those who are called according to his purpose" (Romans 8:28 ESV).

- "I pray that out of his glorious riches he may strengthen you with power through his Spirit in your inner being, so that Christ may dwell in your hearts through faith. And I pray that you, being rooted and established in love, may have power, together with all the Lord's holy people, to grasp how wide and long and high and deep is the love of Christ" (Ephesians 3:16-18 NIV).

- "God can do anything, you know—far more than you could ever imagine or guess or request in your wildest dreams!" (Ephesians 3:20 The Message).

In the midst of sour disappointment, we should not run from God in anger. We should to run to Him. He is the One with the plans for our life, who better to ask for direction and understanding? Even when we feel let down, strong women of God press in and hold on to His promises and the truth of His loving character. We must trust that God has a greater plan and can use <u>ALL</u> the experiences, all the ups, and all the downs of this life for His glory, for our good, and for the good of those we will reach in the future. One of the greatest prayers I started uttering during this time is written below. In times of disappointment, I challenge you to revisit this prayer.

<u>*Prayer Starter*</u>*: God I do not like this season. It's lonely. It hurts. It's uncomfortable, but help me to get whatever it is that You are trying to show me out of this chapter in my journey. I know You do not waste one experience or disappointment in my life. You are powerful enough to use it for my good and for Your Glory. Thank You for being a friend that sticks closer than a brother during this time. Comfort me. Give me hope as I follow Your lead the rest of the way. I trust You and Your plans for my life!*

24. The Tipping Point

FINDING GOD-BALANCE IN LIFE

1 Peter 5:8-9 (AMP) "Be sober [well balanced and self-disciplined], be alert and cautious at all times. That enemy of yours, the devil, prowls around like a roaring lion [fiercely hungry], seeking someone to devour."

D o you ever feel like you have so much going on in life that you are about to explode? Do you ever wish you had more downtime to chill, relax, and just simply breathe? The pressure to keep up with everyone and all the activities is very real and it sometimes drives us to a point where we are physically, emotionally, and spiritually unbalanced.

Although finding and maintaining balance in life can be difficult, I want to motivate you to go straight to God and ask Him for the wisdom and grace to do it! Trying out new routines and ways of handling certain situations in our own strength can have us creating so many new rules and regulations that we end up still not enjoying life. However, if we invite God into the process, He will respond. He will show us what to do more of, what to have less of, when to do it, and how to do it! He will show us what habits need to go, what relationships need to grow, and what routines need to slow. God will help you find balance!

Here is why being balanced is so important:

Being unbalanced makes us vulnerable to the attacks of the enemy. There are certain things that God has designed us to need. Some are physical: water, food, sleep, rest, and exercise. Other needs are emotional like laughter, protection, love, respect, and appreciation. The list goes on and on. When any of these needs are missing, we feel more stressed, more irritable, and farther away from God. Being unbalanced causes us to feel lonely, misunderstood, or impatient. It becomes easier to get upset and it is much harder to calm down and recover if we do explode.

I have noticed that when I do not get enough sleep, I am way less patient and way less kind the next day. When I go a long time without eating, everything and everyone seems to annoy the living day lights out of me. Even my close friends say they know not to even talk to me until I get some food in my stomach! Ha! Other times, I find myself unbalanced when I choose to work over spending quality time with my family and friends. I love to work hard because I love the results. But it is important for me to have a social outlet so I can remember that God has called me to love and nurture my relationships with the people He has placed in my life. He has called me to be loved by them as well. Community and fellowship are needs.

Without balance, we cannot function at our best! This is when the enemy has a party! He will use our attitudes and our mood swings to wreak havoc on our friendships, to make us lose confidence in who we are, and to even cause us to feel depressed and isolated. Sometimes he pushes us to the point where we lose hope and passion for the things we once enjoyed.

But oh, precious one, keep running to God! There are great benefits when we find balance in Him!

BALANCE leads to BLESSING! In different seasons your priorities will change. As a result, it is wise to ask God how to spend your time. Everything will not always deserve equal time, so He will highlight certain commitments that need to become more important than others. He will show you what relationships are not fruitful and therefore deserve less of your energy and focus. Other times, He will nudge you to invest more time in specific friends or family members. The key is to take time to listen to God and actually respond once He speaks. He is a loving Father and He wants to position us for success.

1 Peter 5:10 (ESV) encourages us: "And after you have suffered a little while, the God of all grace, who has called you to his eternal glory in Christ, will himself restore, confirm, strengthen, and establish you."

"Grace" means favor and blessing! To "establish" means to make you what you ought to be. To complete means "to perfect!" I do not know about you, but I want to be a woman who walks in God's favor and blessing! I want God to make me all He wants me to be. I want Him to perfect me as His magnificent creation and as His daughter! Determine to be a woman of balance today! Balance leads to blessing!

Prayer Starter: Dear Heavenly Father, it's me! I am feeling unbalanced and I need Your help to find my peace and happiness again. I know that You created life for me to enjoy, so please help me learn how to best spend my time. Show me what activities I should be involved in and the ones of which I should let go. Show me which relationships to nurture and those I need to release. Reveal what habits and routines are not fruitful and grant me the wisdom to live a better way. I want to operate at optimal capacity for Your glory! Grant me the grace I need! I love You and believe You hear me!

25. Breakthrough is for Warriors

PUSHING THROUGH TO GREATNESS

1 Timothy 6:12 (NLT) "Fight the good fight for the true faith. Hold tightly to the eternal life to which God has called you, which you have confessed so well before many witnesses."

It is always easier to start than to finish. When we begin new years, new projects, new classes, new goals, motivation just seems to flow right out of us. Our hopes are high and our expectations are lofty! Those first few days and even sometimes weeks are full of believing for the impossible and striving for the unimaginable. We even go public with it, declaring to the world: "I am going to do this! Watch and hear me roar!" Everyone cheers and claps to root us on! Yes, oh yes! The beginning of a new venture is oh so exciting!

As the days turn into long nights and our dreams begin to look like miniature sailboats adrift a vast shore, our once eager pursuit can begin to dwindle into a lackluster quest, an indifferent funk, and sometimes even a depression. The temptation to procrastinate gets real and our confidence to achieve our goals begins to fade.

If we were regular chicks, we would have to settle for this cycle. However, because we are Daughters of the Most High God, we have a supernatural power inside of us to rise above the status quo and become all that God created us to be!

When you are losing faith and tired of fighting the battle, hold on to these five P's!

#1 Persistence: Life can get emotional, but we never have to be subject to our feelings. It is okay to be real about not wanting to do something. However, when it is all said and done, strong women of God choose to do what they know they should do even when they do not feel like it. If we remain persistent, God will walk us into victory at just the right time. The struggle helps us appreciate our success even more.

#2 Patience: Trust God's timing. A lot of times when we have dreams and aspirations, we usually want everything to happen now. Sometimes we think we are ready to go to the next level. Other times we get tired of the day-to-day grind, all the obstacles, and all the hurdles. But, my dear sister, hold on! God knows just when to bless us. Let's be determined not to take shortcuts to fulfill our desires. Let's wait on God. Let's stick to the plan. Let's endure to the finish. Waiting on God allows us time to mature enough to handle, rather than forfeit, the blessing.

#3 Process: Have you ever made a mistake? Awesome!!! Welcome to the club! You are a work in progress. Choose to view every day as an opportunity to learn, to grow, and to get better. Strive to be excellent, not perfect. God chooses imperfect people, so He can get the glory. If we were perfect, why would we need Him? When you live with a mindset of excellence, that simply means you make a decision to do your best and let God do the rest! Remember: Life is a process!

#4 Perspective: If you find yourself in a position where you are drained or unmotivated, oftentimes a change in perspective helps. Sometimes we get so caught up in chasing after the things we want that we forget to enjoy where we are. When you feel less than enthused, take some time to sit down and chat with an encouraging friend. Sometimes getting out in the community and serving others will refresh you as well. Do what it takes to reinvigorate yourself and keep going.

#5 Prayer: Our first line of defense in the battles of life should be talking to God in prayer. He is the Ultimate Strategist. He holds the plans for your life in His Hands. Who better to talk to than Him? Prayer allows our hearts to be aligned with God's will for our life. Prayer empowers us to fulfill our destiny. Prayer also gives us wisdom and strength that is essential for breakthrough. The most powerful way to fight through tough times is on our knees in submission to God.

Because life is full of falls, epic fails, and errors, as a fierce woman of God, you have to get really good at getting back up again! God has created you to be an overcomer! A warrior for Christ! The sooner you learn to stop dwelling on your mistakes and fearing the unknowns of life, the quicker you will reach your God-given destiny. Why push through life alone? Remember: God is on this journey with you. Lean on Him and you will breakthrough to greatness!

Prayer Starter: *Dear Heavenly Father, in Your power I can do all things! I declare I will be persistent, patient, and prayerful in every season of my life. I choose to enjoy the process and to embrace the journey. I know that if I do my best and give my all, You will fill in every where that I lack. Help me to keep a good perspective in life and trust that You will get me where I need to be right on time. Every day I am breaking through to greatness!*

26. Stepping Out of the Boat

LEARNING TO DO IT AFRAID!

Joshua 1:9 (NIV) "Have I not commanded you? Be strong and courageous. Do not be afraid; do not be discouraged, for the LORD your God will be with you wherever you go."

Being courageous is a choice. It is one I have to make on a daily basis.

My most amazing victories in life have come when I was downright scared, but made a decision to push through and grab a hold of what God had for me. As I look back on my life, I shudder to think of the incredible experiences, friends, and influence I would not have if I had given into the endless temptations to run away in fear. As I keep making decisions to be brave and face fear head on, I see the consequences are always greater than I could have imagined.

Just like with my life, God wants to use your story for His glory. God writes the most amazing scripts and storylines for our lives, but I believe that sometimes we allow fear to keep us from experiencing some of the best scenes.

I will never forget the day I decided I wanted to compete for the title of Miss America. Even though my big sister had won Miss Chicago, Miss Illinois, and was the first runner-up to Miss America, I had never done a pageant in my life! I remember being 12, watching her get all dolled up in glitzy gowns, hair, and makeup, but I grew up as a tomboy jock whose life revolved around being a volleyball player 24/7. Here I was, now age 23, with just one year of eligibility, one chance, to compete for the coveted crown.

Fearful thoughts bombarded my mind: "You don't even know how to put on makeup! When was the last time you wore heels? You have to perform in front of people! You are shy! What will your friends think? Other girls have more experience—they've done this for years! You're not going to fit in. What if you don't win? You're going to look so stupid!"

The fear was nearly paralyzing. I found myself in tears and anxious at just the thought of telling my loved ones. For weeks I kept my idea a secret; but, for motivation I would watch videos of old Miss America pageants every day. My excitement and courage began to build. I saw what outstanding role models the contestants were! I saw them empowering kids around the nation and speaking on important topics. I saw them using the scholarship money they won to better their education and I read about how successful they became as business women, doctors, lawyers, and nonprofit leaders. I was sufficiently impressed and inspired! I wanted to have this incredible experience for myself!

I knew right then I had a choice to make: Was I going to let my fear or my passion fuel this decision in my life? I could walk away and be comfortable or I could sprint towards my dream. *God gave me the strength to be courageous!* He showed me this opportunity could open up doors in my future and serve as a platform to positively impact others. That day I took the first step and entered a local pageant competition.

The next week I began training with my sister. She taught me how to walk in an evening gown, deliver a compelling interview, and captivate an audience with my stage presence. Instead of letting fear drive me, I started using it to my advantage! When I felt inadequate and insecure, I did not allow myself to get overwhelmed. I learned to take a moment to breathe and identify exactly what I needed to improve upon. Then, I made a plan to do it and I got to it!

This would be the first time I ever sang by myself in public, so I signed up for professional voice lessons. Growing up I sang in choirs, but I shied away from solos and conveniently placed my timid self in the back of the pews for our concerts.

As I kept praying, practicing and preparing, my confidence grew. I learned to trust God with my weaknesses and let Him make my crooked places straight. I knew if I could give my best, God would do the rest!

Three months later, He did just that! I stepped on the stage and God showed up! That night I won the very first pageant of my life and walked away with the title of Miss Houston 2014! To put the icing on the cake, I also won the Talent Award for singing, the Interview Award, and the People's Choice Award! Not a bad start for a rookie competitor!

God has the best of the world in store for you! Make a decision today to be courageous! Remember: With God, all things are possible! (see Matthew 19:26b).

Prayer Starter: _Dear Heavenly Father, when I am afraid, strengthen me with courage! When I doubt, give me faith! I want to take a hold of all that Jesus died for me to have. I want all You have in store for me. Help me to push past fear, so You can use my story for Your glory!_

27. The Gift of Loneliness

EMBRACING SOLITUDE

James 2:23 (ESV) "and the Scripture was fulfilled that says, 'Abraham believed God, and it was counted to him as righteousness'—and he was called a friend of God."

Have you ever found yourself in a room full of people, yet you still felt alone? (I have). Have you ever desperately needed a friend to talk to, a shoulder to cry on, yet out of every last friend you called, not one picks up the stinkin' phone? (I have). Oh, here is a good one: have you ever been the only single person in the midst of a bunch of happy-go-lucky couples? (Awkward...but yes, I have). I think it is safe to say we have all been in at least one of these positions, where "riding solo" ain't so fun. However, one of the most empowering mindsets you can have is one that welcomes and embraces moments of solitude and seasons of loneliness.

Whether it was in high school, college, or even my young adult life, I have had many, maaannnyyy seasons where it has been just me and God. Although it has been extremely tough and lonely at times, I would not trade one of these seasons even if you paid me.

Here is why:

<u>Seasons of Solitude Have Been God's Way of Protecting Me</u>: I will never forget the night I broke down crying to my sister out of frustration that I had no friends in high school. Between my freshman and sophomore year I had moved from Arizona to Texas, so it felt like I was starting all over again. I had left all my best friends and teammates behind and found it hard to meet other students who shared my same interests and values. New state. New cultures. New schools. New teams . . . New opportunities to feel like a loner. It seemed like everyone had their crew and none of them were accepting new members.

At the time I felt rejected, but now I realize I was protected. I see now that God was keeping me from peers who would have negatively influenced my character and outlook on life. Many of the kids I thought I wanted to befriend ended up dealing with drugs, gangs, and/or becoming sexually active at an early age. If we had been hanging out, I may have been tempted to join in on their behaviors to fit in—a decision that could have altered my future. Thank God He saw the larger picture.

Seasons of Loneliness Have Been God's Way of Preserving Me: In my twenties I developed a huge crush on a guy at church. He was great: tall, dark, and handsome. He was in love with God and passionately focused on pursuing his purpose in Christ. For months I prayed that God would give us a chance to get to know each other and develop a solid friendship. For a while, literally everywhere I went in church, there he was. I enjoyed our impromptu conversations. The more we talked, the more I wanted to see him. Soon I was putting extra effort into the way I dressed. I wanted to look my absolute best just in case I saw him. Then during the service I would look around to see if I could spot him. I knew I should not allow myself to be distracted, so if he walked by I would desperately pray: "Lord Jesus, please help me focus! Give me the strength and discipline to center my attention on You right now." Still, my heart and mind remained divided and distracted.

All of a sudden, it was like God flipped a switch: I began to rarely see him. To make matters worse, the guy started acting awkward and literally WALKING AWAY from me. We had not talked in weeks yet the poor guy seemed straight up scared of me. It was as if God Himself came down and told him to "STAY

AWAY!!!" It was the most painful lesson I had to learn and one that took me a couple of good cries to get over.

Yet again, I can now look back and see that God's plans were far greater than mine. This crush came at a very crucial season in my life when God was calling me to focus on my career transition and special projects he had placed on my heart. In order to be a good steward of the ideas and opportunities God was giving to me, I needed to be 100% focused on Him, not a man. God wanted my time and energy channeled into doing His work and this could not have happened if I was emotionally entangled with someone. Moreover, this guy had similar passions. During our chats, he would give me very sound advice on how to pursue my goals, but his suggestions did not align with the direction that God was giving me. I was risking mishandling God's mission for my life, a mission that would impact other people. Thank God He blocked it!

God can speak powerfully through people and He can touch us mightily in the context of community, but there is nothing that will ever compare to one-on-one, intimate, and personal time with Him. Seasons of solitude position us in a place where we are free from distractions and influences that cloud our judgment and negatively affect our ability to make godly decisions.

It is hard to understand sometimes why we have to go through these times of loneliness, but we have to trust that God knows best: **Isaiah 55:9 (NLT) says: "For just as the heavens are higher than the earth, so my ways are higher than your ways and my thoughts higher than your thoughts."** The sooner we learn to go with God's plan, the easier life will be. He has the big picture in mind and He knows the entirety of His plans for our life.

If you are in a place of solitude right now, my advice to you is: *Surrender.* Choose to embrace this time as an opportunity to hear God's heart and to get to know Him better. Choose to believe that He is protecting you and preparing you for the great plans He has ahead.

Prayer Starter: Dear Heavenly Father, I declare that You are in charge! I surrender! Take the wheel and help me let go of it! When I go through seasons of loneliness, help me to understand that You are not punishing me, but protecting me. Give me the wisdom to stop fighting Your will, and start trusting Your ways. I want to know no other person more intimately than I know You. Take me deep into Your Love and Friendship!

28. What's in Your Pantry?

STORING UP ON GOD

Romans 10:17 (NIV) "Consequently, faith comes from hearing the message, and the message is heard through the word about Christ."

When you live in Houston, Texas a while you learn very quickly to take hurricane season seriously. When the weather man starts pointing at that white swirling figure on the radar moving into the Gulf Coast, you know things are about to get real! If you have not stocked your pantry, you'd better pray it is not too late! Folks go nuts racing to the grocery stores to buy everything from water to bread to flashlights. Sometimes the hurricane turns its course and showers us with light rain; other times, it leaves a devastating and lasting imprint that takes lives and ruins homes. It is during seasons like these that some brave soul refuses to heed the warning. They ride on the idea of luck, denying the need to prepare, hoping to skate by yet another year. Oftentimes, their story ends in unnecessary tragedy or loss.

Just like we do not wait to get prepared for life's emergencies, we cannot wait until our spiritual life is under attack to get serious about our walk with God. Our spirit is like a pantry that needs to be constantly stocked and replenished. The Bible, also known as the Word of God, is the food we need to fill our souls. God is always loving and gracious enough to pick us up when we are down, but there are a lot of things we can do beforehand to prepare ourselves for life's inevitable storms. Thanks to technology, there are countless ways to access the Word of God.

5 Ways to Store Up Your Spiritual Pantry

#1 Daily Devotional Time: I love pastors, I love books, I love sermons, I love mentors, and I especially love Christian apps, but nothing can ever replace reading the Word of God for myself. If you have not made it a priority, start reading the

Bible every day. As you begin to read God's Word, you begin to understand what His voice sounds like. This will help you make better decisions throughout your day and give you the wisdom you need to live your best life. I suggest getting a study Bible to help you along. I always feel smarter when I am done reading mine. They explain what you are reading, tell you the history behind the stories, and help you keep everything in context. Many study Bibles often have themes and include short devotionals. I have noticed they cover special topics ranging from sports to dating to leadership. If you cannot remember why setting a devotional time is so important, reread "Girl on a Mission: Starting Your Day Off Strong."

#2 Download a Bible App & Pick a Favorite Translation: With over 550 versions of the Bible available today, technology has taken away the excuse of not being able to understand the Word. You can download Bible applications on your phone and different versions will be at your fingertips. If all of the "thee's" and "thou's" give you a headache, find a contemporary version that is more your style. I usually read the physical Bible at home and use the app for when I am on the go! I love not having to add that extra weight to my purse or backpack.

#3 Devotional Apps & Christian eBooks: I love "snacking" on the Word of God. If I am caught in a long checkout line at the store, I will pull out my phone and read while I wait on other customers to be helped. The time not only passes by, but it also helps my anxious and impatient mood quickly dissipate, as motivation and inspiration from the Word builds my spirit.

#4 Worship Music: Explore YouTube and iTunes to find your favorite Christian band or worship team. I love watching music videos because I am encouraged when I see the millions of other believers around the world who are on this spiritual journey with us. It is uplifting to observe their passion for God. Just like the people of God are diverse, there are different genres of worship music ranging from Christian hip-hop to alternative. I love them ALL! Just as with Bible translations, you can find whatever type of music fits you. Listen to it when you work out, when you are on the go, or when you are simply chilling at home. Music is food for the soul, especially when it is filled with powerful lyrics from the Word of God.

#5 Online Sermons & Audio Books: Listening to sermons or an audio version of the Bible being read aloud is another great way to store up good food in your spirit. You can buy a recording of a sermon, find one online, or download an app from your favorite pastor. I love to listen to the Word as I get ready in the morning or when I clean my room. The time flies by much faster that way!

Pastor John Osteen, the founder of Lakewood Church in Houston, Texas, always said: "Put the Word in you when you don't need it, so that it will be in you when you do need it." The more we feed on the Word of God, the more it will become a part of the way we think and speak. It will begin to change the way you act towards others and the way you respond to unexpected situations.

Lastly, remember this: *Strong women of God don't get ready; we stay ready!* When the hurricane seasons of life come, we will not have to panic! We will be prepared for any and every emergency the world throws at us when our spiritual pantries are filled up with God's Word.

Prayer Starter: Dear Heavenly Father, thank You for the gift of the Word! I know there is no book more powerful than the Bible itself. Help me to be disciplined and creative about storing up on the Word in every season of life. I desire to be ready for all life has in store for me!

29. Rain or Shine

IN IT TO WIN IT!

Philippians 4:11-13 (ISV) "I am not saying this because I am in any need, for I have learned to be content in whatever situation I am in. I know how to be humble, and I know how to prosper. In each and every situation I have learned the secret of being full and of going hungry, of having too much and of having too little. I can do all things through Him who strengthens me."

E verybody likes a good sunny day. These are the days in life when all you do is win! Everything is going great: you ace the test, you are at peace with your friends and family, and you not only look good, but you also feel great! Life seems to have a nice forecast of clear blue skies and open doors ahead. Oh, yes! The sunny seasons of life are just plain fun! The rainy days, on the other hand, are the ones you would rather do without. This is when life gets tough: a relationship goes sour, a dream is shattered, or something you hope for is delayed. These are the moments you wish would pass by quickly. It reminds me of the song, *The Itsy Bitsy Spider*...

"Out came the sun and dried up all the rain

And the itsy bitsy spider climbed up the spout again...."

Wouldn't it be nice if the rainy days would go away that easily? Unfortunately, often these days become rainy months and those months turn into rainy seasons. The longer they last, the harder it can be to get ourselves out of a rut of negativity and depression. In rainy times, it can be tempting to fall into disobedience and lose hope. But, girl! You have got to push! Push through the thunder, the lightening, the wind, and the rain. Like the saying goes: "When the going gets tough, the tough get going!" How will you respond in the stormy seasons of life?

Truthfully speaking, there should not be a difference between how we operate in the good or the bad times. None of us would remain friends with someone who enjoyed our company one day, but ignored us the next day. Even Jesus says in **Revelation 3:15 (NLT): "I know all the things you do, that you are** neither hot nor cold. I wish that you were one or the other!" Just like we do not want wishy-washy friends, why would we expect God to be any different?

Be committed to your spiritual walk with God. Be in it to win it! If you can press through the rainy days of life, remaining consistent, faithful, and obedient, God will not only give you rainbows, but He will also prepare pots of gold!

Sometimes that gold comes in the form of an <u>attitude upgrade</u>. Rainy days have a way of showing you just how grateful, how kind, how patient, and how loving you *really* are when things are not going your way. At first you may not welcome God's attitude checks, but eventually you will get excited about them. When God works on your attitude, He is about to take you higher! He promotes women of character and humility that He can trust to represent Him well, those women who will give Him the glory when they reach their next level of success. Do not get caught with a bad attitude during the storm. Be grateful. Be patient. Know deep in your heart that God corrects those He loves (see Hebrews 12:6) . . . and He loves YOU!

Other times that "gold" looks like a <u>change in perspective</u>. Let's face it! Sometimes we can be hard-headed. In my life, I learned best on the rainy days when God took opportunities away from me, when He blocked a relationship I wanted, or when He seemed to take a long time to answer a prayer. At first I would kick and scream, sometimes cry and even get mad. I would tell God all about how I thought the situation was unfair or how I "deserved" something. The truth is, God did not owe me anything and He usually gave me several warnings beforehand to let go of something or someone. It was not until He took what I desired away that I realized I was distracted, putting myself in danger, or wasting my time. Once I had that distraction out of my life, I gained fresh perspective. With a fresh perspective comes joy, energy, wisdom, and productivity that is priceless. Clear skies!!!

The way you respond in the midst of a storm can dramatically transform your life for the better. When you know God is the only person Who will ever have your back 100% of the time, you begin to trust Him and His ways regardless of how you feel. You begin to understand that He uses the good, the bad, and the ugly times just the same. If you are in a rainy season, ask God to clear your vision. Ask Him to help you learn and grow. Ask Him for the strength to thrive and not just to survive. If you are going to experience the storm, you might as well get something out of it! Be determined to press through the rainy days and come out bearing pots of gold! Remember: Even plants cannot survive on sunshine alone. They need rain to grow.

Prayer Starter: Dear Heavenly Father, You have made me a fierce woman of God. Equip me with the strength and wisdom I need to get through this tough time. Please help me to remain constant in times of trial. I want to be faithful to You, consistent in my obedience, and dedicated to walking out Your will for my life. I know that You do what is best for me. When I put my trust in You, I will always win.

30. Keeping the Big Picture

RELATIONSHIPS ARE WORTH FIGHTING FOR

Ephesians 6:10-12 (NASB) "Finally, be strong in the Lord and in the strength of His might. Put on the full armor of God, so that you will be able to stand firm against the schemes of the devil. For our struggle is not against flesh and blood, but against the rulers, against the powers, against the world forces of this darkness, against the spiritual forces of wickedness in the heavenly places."

M̲ake no mistake: when you argue with a loved one, the devil is jumping for joy. Do not imagine for a moment that when you part ways with a good friend the devil is saddened by the fallout. In fact, as evil as it sounds, he rejoices in it! **The Bible tells us that Satan "comes only to steal and kill and destroy" (John 10:10 NIV).** The main thing he loves to ruin is our relationships. As strong women of God, we must get really good at guarding our hearts and protecting our inner circles from the work of this vicious and cunning enemy. He is relentless! We should be too!

As I discussed in "Who's in Your Squad?: Choosing Friends Wisely", there will be times in life when you have to prayerfully disconnect and let go of friends who are a bad influence on you. However, just because we find a relationship challenging, does not always mean we get a free pass to let them go! Sometimes the most difficult relationships in life are the ones most worth fighting for!

One of the most challenging relationships I have experience in my life is with my very own mother. When I returned to Houston from living on my own in college, I thought I was going to pull my hair out! It seemed like we were different in every single way possible. My mom was very carefree, very easygoing, and she had a knack for enjoying even the simplest pleasures in life. I, on the other hand, was very uptight. Being fresh on the scene as a young adult out of school, I had major plans about where I wanted to be in five years and I was taking no prisoners. I was strict about my schedule, I took little time for entertainment; and, I was stressing myself out about my goals and aspirations constantly. I wanted to "be somebody!"

As you can imagine, my mother and I clashed . . . A LOT! I could never understand how she could live life so relaxed and she found it difficult to sympathize with my stress. After months of discord, I finally realized we were not going to make it this way. In tears, I brought it to God:

I prayed that God would help us get along. I prayed that He would help me respect her. I prayed that we would never argue again and that He would keep us from nagging one another. I would love to tell you that God healed everything in one day. I wish I could write about how miraculously smooth our relationship became once I got on my knees in prayer, but I'd be lying.

This was a relationship I would have to continually fight for. It has now been four years since I graduated from college. What I can tell you is that in this time, as I desperately leaned on God, He has used this relationship to make me better in every way:

God Uses Relationships to Build Character: One Sunday was an especially awesome day of ministering at church. I was all smiles and a delight to be around as I welcomed folks into the sanctuary and prayed for them after the service. I will never forget wanting to get straight home and use the inspiration from the sermon to start working towards my goals for the week when my mother announces that she needed to run a couple of errands. What became a "few stops" took at least two hours. As you might have guessed, I became irritated. I tried to stay calm, but everything in me was so annoyed. In that moment, God convicted me: "How could you act so lovely and pleasant at church, yet you leave the building and act like a monster?" I began to realize that God wanted me to be the same woman I was in public as I was in private.

For the last few years now, this has stayed on my mind as I continuously work toward this goal. Someone once said that we often feel like we can treat loved ones differently than we do friends because we know they will not leave us. However, as women of integrity, we should respect and love the ones God has placed in our family <u>the most</u>. Truly, these are the relationship that are worth the fight!

God Uses Relationships to Broaden Your Perspective: Rather than rolling my eyes when my mother would encourage me to "relax" or "calm down," I have learned to listen to her wisdom. Instead of taking offense, I now take it as a cue from God that I need to make sure I am balanced in life. Being ambitious is great, but our goals should never consume us. My mother is a constant reminder to enjoy the journey of life while moving toward the destination.

God Uses Relationships to Strengthen Your Prayer Life: Certain things in life have simple solutions and quick fixes; but, when it comes to people, only God can influence their hearts. This is why prayer is key! **Ezekiel 36:36 (HCSB) says: "I will give you a new heart and put a new spirit within you; I will remove your heart of stone and give you a heart of flesh."** This scripture perfectly captures what I have experienced! Rather than changing my mother or my situation, God changed ME! When I wanted to give up, He has kept my heart from hardening and becoming cold towards her when I wanted to give up. As a result, He has been able to strengthen our relationship and make us better as we pursue unity and harmony in our life.

The enemy wants to destroy relationships that you need in your life. I would not be as successful without the direction of my mother and her wisdom. This is a relationship he would love to ruin because no one can speak into my life like she can. No one knows me inside and out like she does and no one believes in me like she will. After all, she is my mother! If you are struggling with a valuable relationship like this, go to God in prayer! Don't wait! Keep the bigger picture and refuse to let the enemy win! It is a relationship worth fighting for!

Prayer Starter: _Dear Heavenly Father, forgive me for hardening my heart and giving up on people when things get hard. Give me the strength and patience to especially love and respect my family. Please cover and protect my inner circle from the schemes of the enemy. I want to value those who You have strategically placed in my life. Grant me discernment in my relationships and help me to always lead with prayer and love._

31. Forgiven & Free

NEVER TOO JACKED UP FOR JESUS

John 3:16 (NIV) "For God so loved the world that he gave his one and only Son, that whoever believes in him shall not perish but have eternal life."

When God put this world into motion, He said: "It is good!" When Jesus' last drop of blood hit the ground, He declared: "It is finished!" What God declares is truth. What Jesus did on the cross is final! Unlike human beings, God cannot lie. Unlike us, God does not second guess Himself, mess up, or take back what He says. In the same way, when God created you, He declared: "She is good!" When He sent His Son Jesus to die on the cross, He did it with YOU in mind. Take that personally today! God not only declares that you are a wonderful creation, but you are also FORGIVEN and completely FREE!!!

Since the earth was put into motion, people could never get it right 100% of the time. Although God planned for us to enjoy life, worship Him, and live free of worries, cares, and burdens, it did not take long for Adam and Eve to mess up that deal. Their disobedience invited sin into the world and changed everything for generations to come. God sent the Ten Commandments, many different priests, kings, queens, prophets, and leaders to try to guide His people back to His heart and original design for their lives. But, they were not able to uphold God's standard. Plus, just like any other human being, these well-meaning leaders also had flaws of their own. Back then, when people messed up or sinned, the punishment was oftentimes death. For example, if a person committed adultery they were stoned to death. If a child or slave made a mistake, they were flogged (beaten, whipped). In order to avoid these harsh penalties, they sacrificed an unblemished animal as a substitute. But thank God for JESUS!

Because of Jesus, we do not have to endure all of this today. We do not have to make sacrifices or be physically punished for our sins. Nope! God being so gracious and merciful, took matters into His own Hands. God sent His Son Jesus and empowered Him through the Holy Spirit to live a perfect, sinless life. He became the new unblemished sacrifice. When Jesus died on the cross, His death covered every sin that we have committed and will ever commit in the future! Jesus paid the price so that we would have the chance to be reconnected to God and live the life He originally planned for us, including dwelling with Him for eternity!

Now you and I can live freely today! When we sin, we can simply ask God for forgiveness. When we struggle, we can easily ask Jesus to help us live like He lived. When we need strength, wisdom, and discipline, we can ask the Holy Spirit to guide us and give us knowledge.

I want you to trust and hold on to God's forgiveness and freedom today! Life can get so hard that sometimes we end up feeling too messed up for God to use us. We feel like our mistakes are too big, our weaknesses too many, and our sins too awful. We feel like we have run so far away from God that He would never want us back or that He would not waste His time trying to catch us. But my dear friend, these thoughts could not be further from the truth (see Romans 8:14-17).

GOD CAN NEVER STOP LOVING YOU!
GOD WILL ALWAYS BE CHASING YOU!
GOD IS LOVE and GOD LOVES YOU!

As a strong woman of God, I need you to get this in your spirit. Life will knock you down, sin will creep in, and you will mess up, but you must know that God's hand is always reaching out to pull you back up. ALWAYS! **Proverbs 24:16 (AMP) says: "For a righteous man falls seven times, and rises again, [b]ut the wicked stumble in *time of* disaster *and* collapse."** Mighty girl, when you fall, you have to get good at getting back up again!

To be righteous means to be RIGHT with God. It means to come to Him openly and honestly confessing your sins, acknowledging that Jesus came to die for YOU, and dedicating yourself to live your life in a way that glorifies and honors what Jesus did on the cross. He not only came to give you eternal life in Heaven, but He also came to give you an awesome life right here, right now, on earth.

Have you received this amazing gift from Him yet? If not, pray about it and consider making this commitment to Jesus today. Maybe you have grown up in church and walked with God for a while. Perhaps today is the day where you make a fresh commitment. I promise you, it will be the best decision you will ever make in your life! You will do far better with God than you could ever do on your own. He created you and has phenomenal plans for your life.

Declare today that you are forgiven, free, and onboard with Jesus!

<u>*Prayer Starter*</u>*: Dear Heavenly Father, thank You for Jesus! Thank You for sending Your one and only Son to die for me and my sins! I choose to take that personally today. Please forgive me for all of my sins, come into my heart, and wash me clean. Make me new again! I declare today that You are my Lord and my Savior. I am never too jacked up for You to use. I am never too far gone for You to catch me. Hold me tight, Lord, and help me*

144

receive Your love like never before. Help me to live a life that is honoring to You! I love You! I declare that I am completely forgiven and free! I AM TOTALLY YOURS! Amen!

ACKNOWLEDGEMENTS

Dr. Fred Jones, J.D (Publish Me Now University): It is very rare that a person finds someone who believes in their dream as much as he or she believes in their own dreams. You are one of those gems. I appreciate every ounce of energy, time, and effort you have put into the development and release of this book. You have poured your heart into this. From start to finish, from conception to delivery, you have been there. For that, sir, I am grateful. Thank you for your patience, your honest feedback, and your support. As my writing coach and publishing strategist, you are Dr. Jones, but forever you will be my "Uncle Fred." I love you like my very own family!

Jonathan Jones (Publish Me Now University): The resources and knowledge you have provided have been key. Thanks for answering my endless list of questions and for always willingly passing along nuggets of wisdom and direction. Appreciate you, "King Jon!"

Pamela-Faye: Wow! Just wow! You are God's gift to me! I could not have dreamt of a more amazing editor. I felt safe, valued, and covered, knowing my book was in your hands. Thank you for using use your gifts and skills to ensure this book would be easily understood by those who read it. Your work was excellent! May God bless you 100-fold!

Loretta Smalls: The only thing better than a praying mother is a praying mother who knows how to edit! You have an eye for quality work! I am amazed by every little mistake you caught.

That attention to detail was so key in producing a product of excellence. Who would have thought that God placed one of the best editors right in my own home? Love you and thank you!

Jerome Smalls: The approval of a father is second-to-none. To have your blessing on this book meant the world to me. You were the very first reader and your feedback gave me the confidence to go forward, knowing this book will bless millions of young women one day. Thank you for believing in me and for always showering me with love.

Jade Simmons: You are my rock! You are also my counselor and personal part-time comedian. Thank you for teaching how to stay true to my mission and my vision. Thank you for making me laugh and for always telling me the truth in love. Your encouragement and wisdom has been vital to this journey. #mogulsinthemaking

Barbara Curtis: Thank you for giving me platforms to share my story. Who would have known that a couple of blogs for RARE Pearls would evolve into this so quickly? Your belief in me means more than you will ever know. You are truly a woman of excellence and one of my greatest role models. God bless you!

Pastor Steve & Suzie Austin: Thank you for sharing your sweet daughter, Lauren, with me! God could not have given me a more perfect family to be the "guinea pigs" for this book. Thank you for being incredible stewards of this project. To have the perspective of a mom, father, pastor, and pastor's wife, all in one couple, was invaluable.

Pastor Michael & Fiona Mellett: Hearing that Celia Kate was enjoying this book gave me the ammunition I needed to keep going. Thank you for allowing me the chance to pour into her life with this book and thank you for so generously pouring into mine. I treasure you two deeply!

Steven Grant (GrantFoto): You did it yet again! You do more than simply take pictures; you capture moments. Your work is untouchable! Thank you for making this book cover shot possible and A-MA-ZING!

Misty Rockwell (Glam Studio by Misty Rockwell): From my very first photo shoot as a pageant contestant to my official Miss Houston photography and now to my very first book cover: You keep a girl lookin' good! REAL good! You are by far one of the best makeup artists to ever walk this planet! Thank you!

ABOUT THE AUTHOR

Within just a few minutes of meeting Isis Smalls you quickly understand why she was touted as one of *Huffington Post's Top 20 Young Movers and Shakers*. From her career as a record-breaking scholar-athlete, to her impacting reign as Miss Houston to her distinctive role as a dedicated 6th Grade Reading & English Teacher, Isis Smalls is an uncommon inspiration in a society in desperate search for dynamic, reliable female role models. She will be releasing her first book for young women entitled "Beauty in the Making: Learning to Radiate from the Inside Out" in the Spring of 2017.

With a stunning combination of brains and brawn, Isis eagerly passes on the winning habits she has developed over a lifetime of limitless living, high-achieving and big dreaming. She powerfully speaks to young girls from all walks of life about the process of unlocking potential and fiercely coaches student-athletes looking to be successful in the game of life: on and off the court.

Prior to her role in the Houston Independent School District, Smalls was an All-American recognized, record-breaking volleyball player and two-time team captain at the 4th-ranked University of Chicago where she earned a full academic scholarship and led her team to the NCAA Tournament for the first time in school history.

The day after graduating, Isis was on a plane to Houston, Texas as a recruit for *Teach for America*, where she has since educated over 350 students in one of the city's underserved communities.

In her second year at the school, she coached her completely novice middle school volleyball team to their first-ever championship win.

Looking to broaden her platform for young girls, Isis expanded her own identity and opportunities outside of sports and education when she was crowned *Miss Houston 2014*, winning her first pageant ever. She also took home the interview and talent awards.

One month into her reign, Isis became the National Ambassador for *Girls in the Game,* a leading non-profit organization in girls' health and fitness. Smalls was later invited as a special guest to the *United Nations International Sport & Social Impact Summit* where she spoke on her strategies for using sports to positively influence young women. In her ambassadorial role, Isis also produced the first *Girls in the Game Interactive,* a city-wide clinic in which 40 Houston-area girls learned about volleyball, field hockey, and nutrition.

Isis went on to place 6th at the Miss Texas Pageant. Since then, Isis has served as the keynote speaker at youth conferences and events, reaching nearly 3,500 young girls with positive messages of empowerment and dreaming big across the nation. She was featured in the *National Public Radio's Secret Lives of Teachers Series* for her accomplishments in the classroom and on the stage.

When she is not speaking, she's singing! She has performed the National Anthem for several high-profile events, most notably for the *Houston Rockets* and the *Association of Tennis Professional's Men's Clay Court Championship* in April 2015.

A committed coach to aspiring, high-achieving student-athletes and a motivator to those looking to raise their level of fitness, Isis is a Certified Personal Trainer with the *National Academy of Sports Medicine.* She uses coaching volleyball as a means to mentor young girls in personal and leadership development, while positioning them to be highly competitive, college-bound athletes and driven women who are passionate about realizing their own potential. Her trainees have gone on to be invaluable, high-scoring leaders on their teams in both the competitive high school and college arenas.

For Isis Smalls, inspiring others into action is her passion. Making a difference is her mode of operation.

www.isissmalls.com

Stay tuned for the release of the

Beauty in the Making: Learning to Radiate from the Inside Out Devotional!

For booking information:

management@isissmalls.com

Get inspiration delivered to your inbox! Sign up for her mailing list:

http://bit.ly/signup4isissmalls

Connect with Isis Smalls on Social Media!

www.isissmalls.com